I0483499

Sundry Art Coloring Book
Pen & Ink Illustrations By Don Kirk

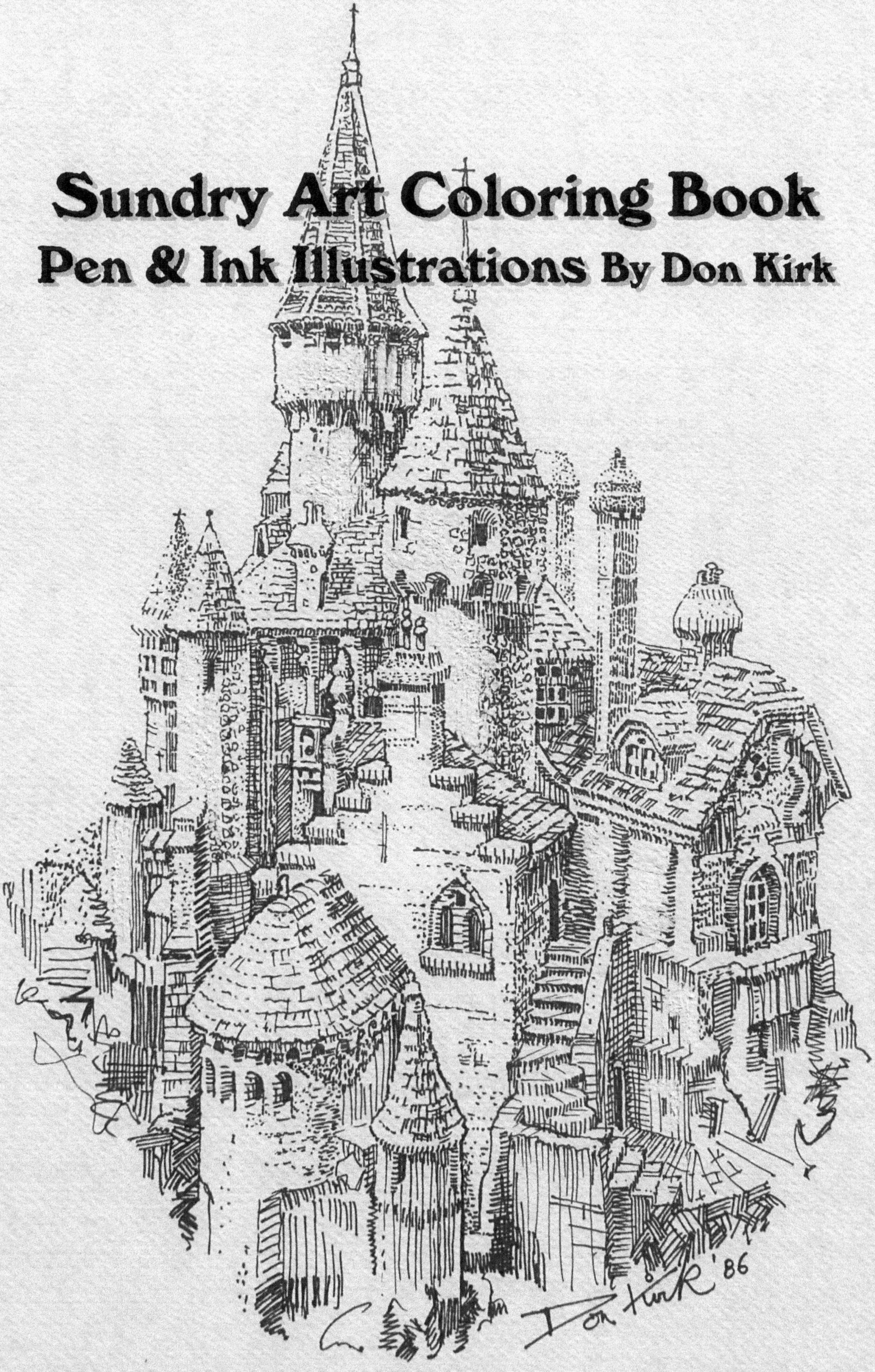

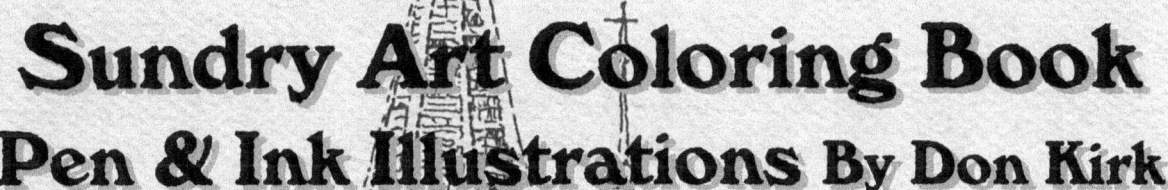

Sundry Art Coloring Book
Pen & Ink Illustrations By Don Kirk

Copyright © Don Kirk 2019
All rights reserved.

No part of this publication may be reproduced, stored in a retrieval
system, or transmitted in any form or by any means, electronic,
mechanical, photocopying, recording, or otherwise, without written
permission of the publisher. For information regarding permission,
email Don Kirk at kirkwest@sbcglobal.net

Published by
SWEETWATER STAGELINES™
An imprint of
THE OLD WEST COMPANY™
5118 Village Trail Drive
San Antonio, Texas 78218

Tradepaper (ISBN13): 978-0-9898004-7-1
Printed and bound in the United States of America

Other Pen & Ink Coloring Books By Don Kirk:
Western Art Coloring Book Volume One
Western Art Coloring Book Volume Two
Iron Horse Art Coloring Book

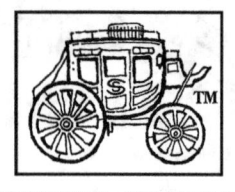

SWEETWATER STAGELINES™
SAN ANTONIO, TEXAS

Sundry Art Coloring Book
Pen & Ink Illustrations By Don Kirk

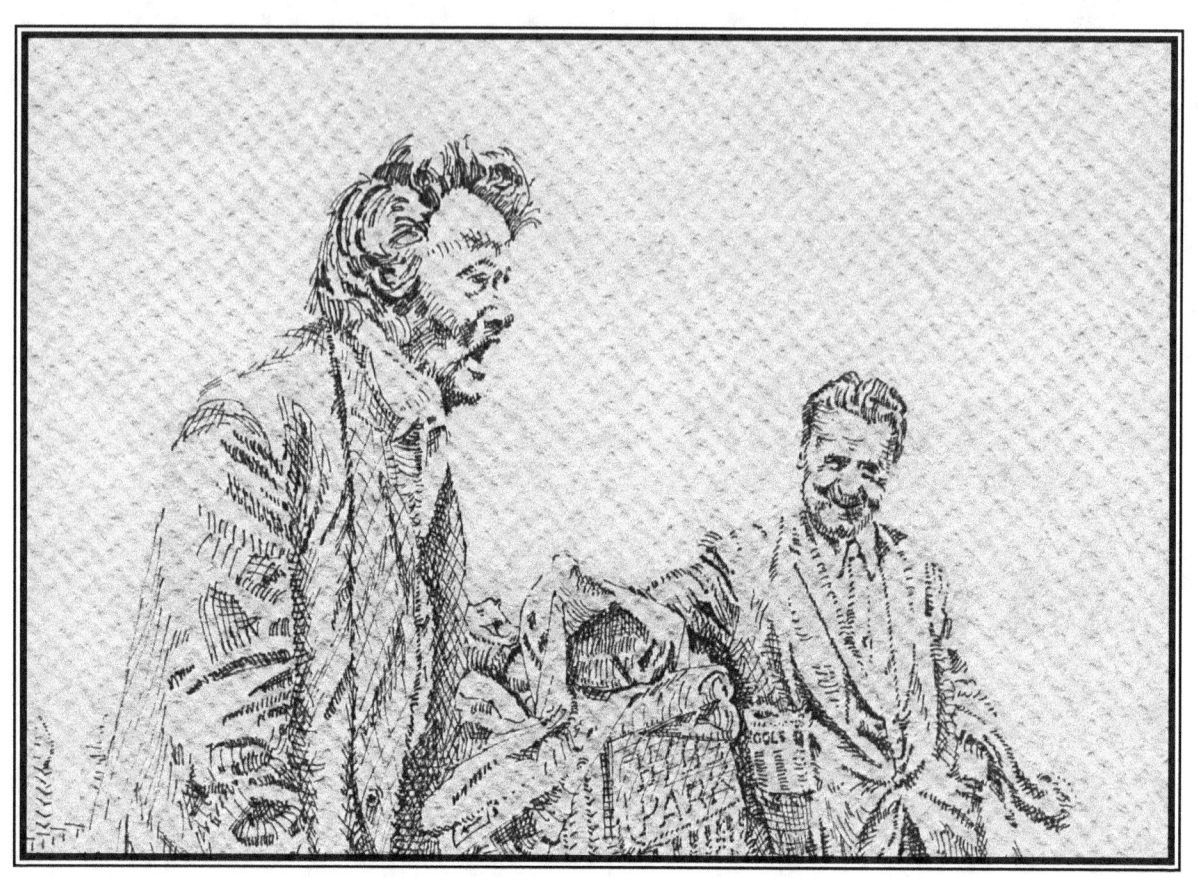

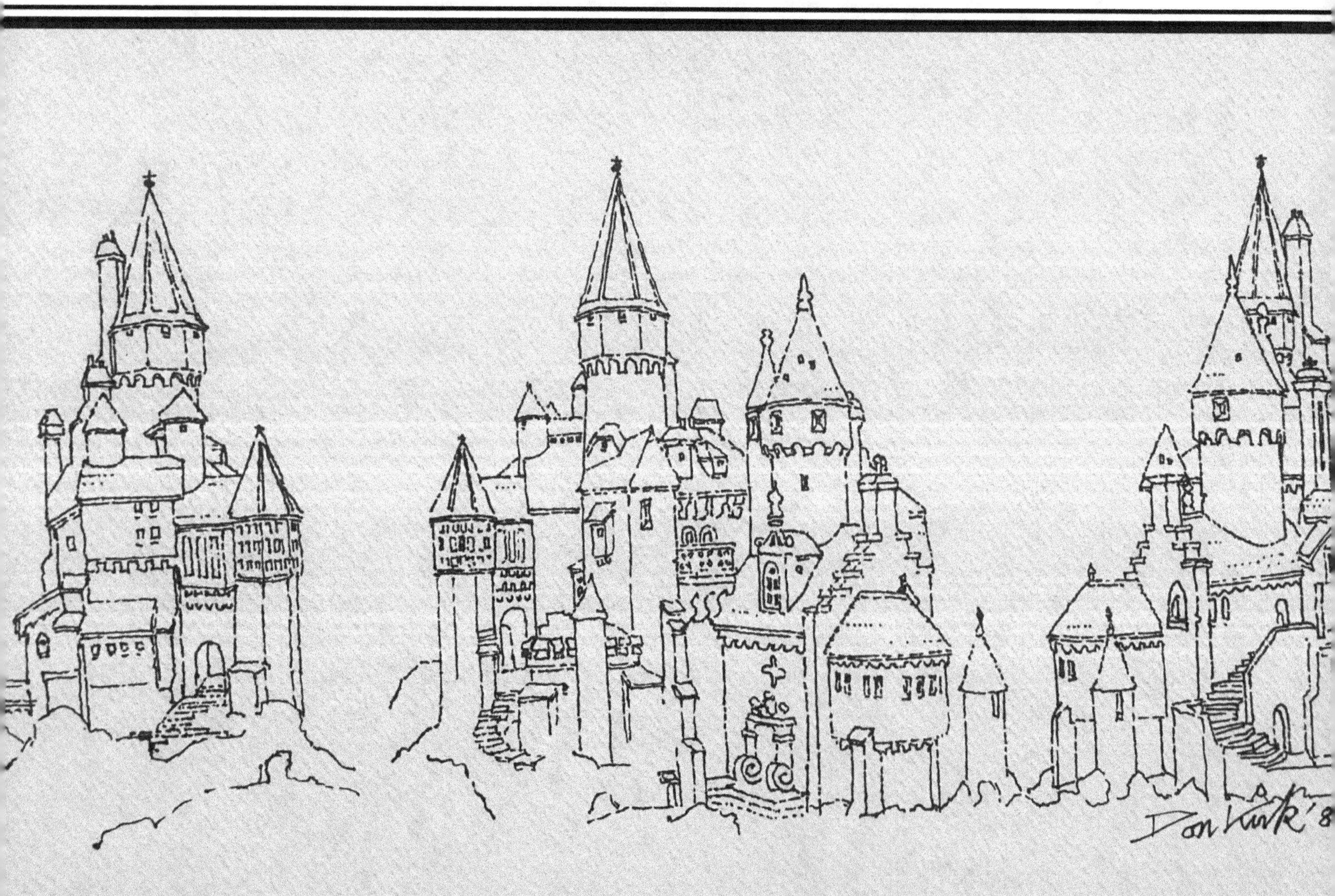

Don Kirk has been drawing in pencil and Pen & Ink as far back as the late 1970's for use on notecards, postcards, advertising brochures, newspaper articles, and art prints and this is the first reproduction of some of these early works of art that can be used for coloring with pencil or crayon or for just framing and looking at. Created for different projects, the only thing shared were the drawing tools; not even the type of paper or its size has any commonality. You'll find a few Medieval castles of Europe, filmmaking artwork, a few historic missions of San Antonio, Texas Independence sketches found on monuments in West Columbia, some backyard artifacts, a medical museum montage, and a couple of western film stars. You can flip through these pages and wonder how they were used and I hope you find this miscellany interesting unto themselves. So Enjoy.

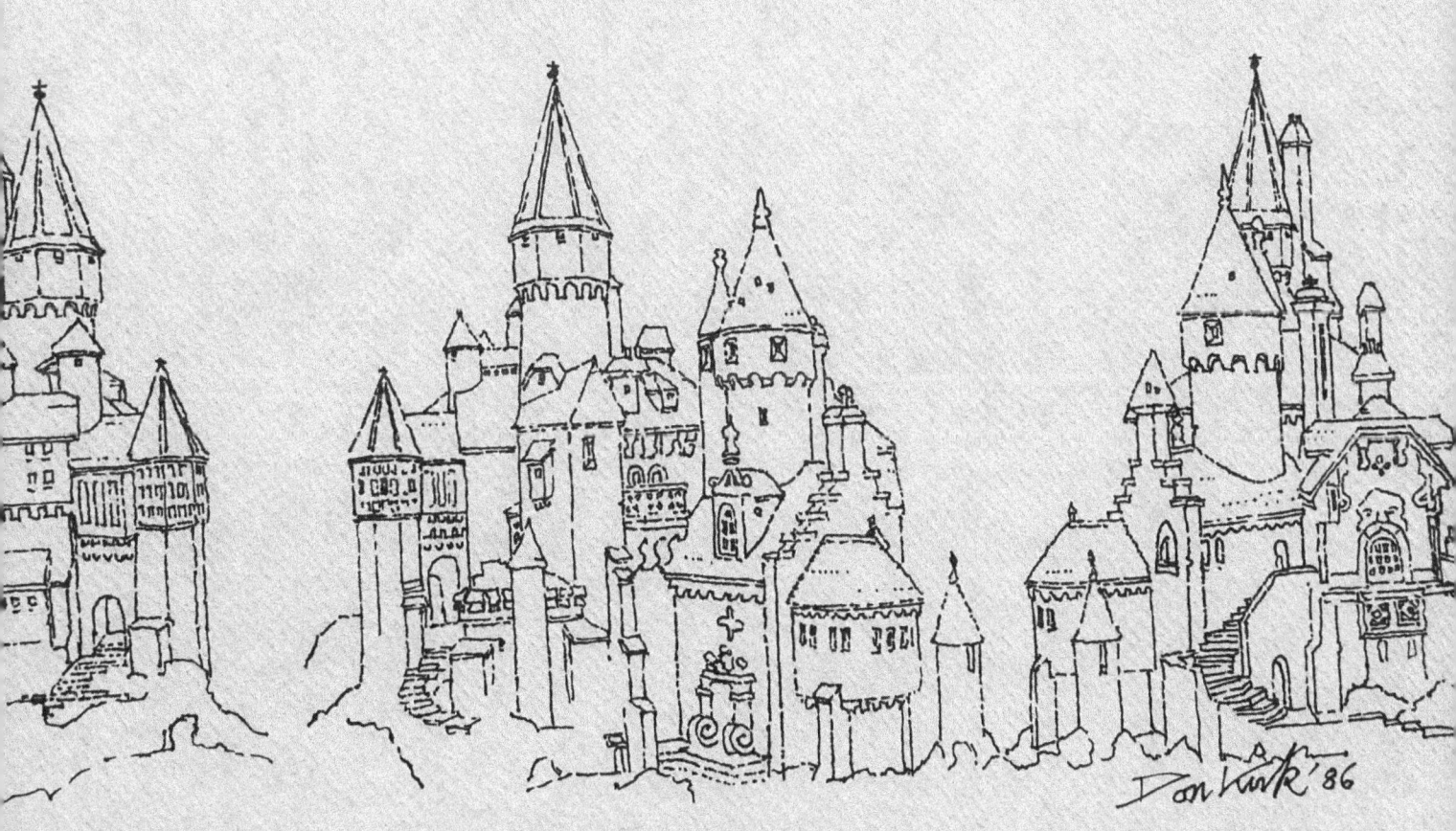

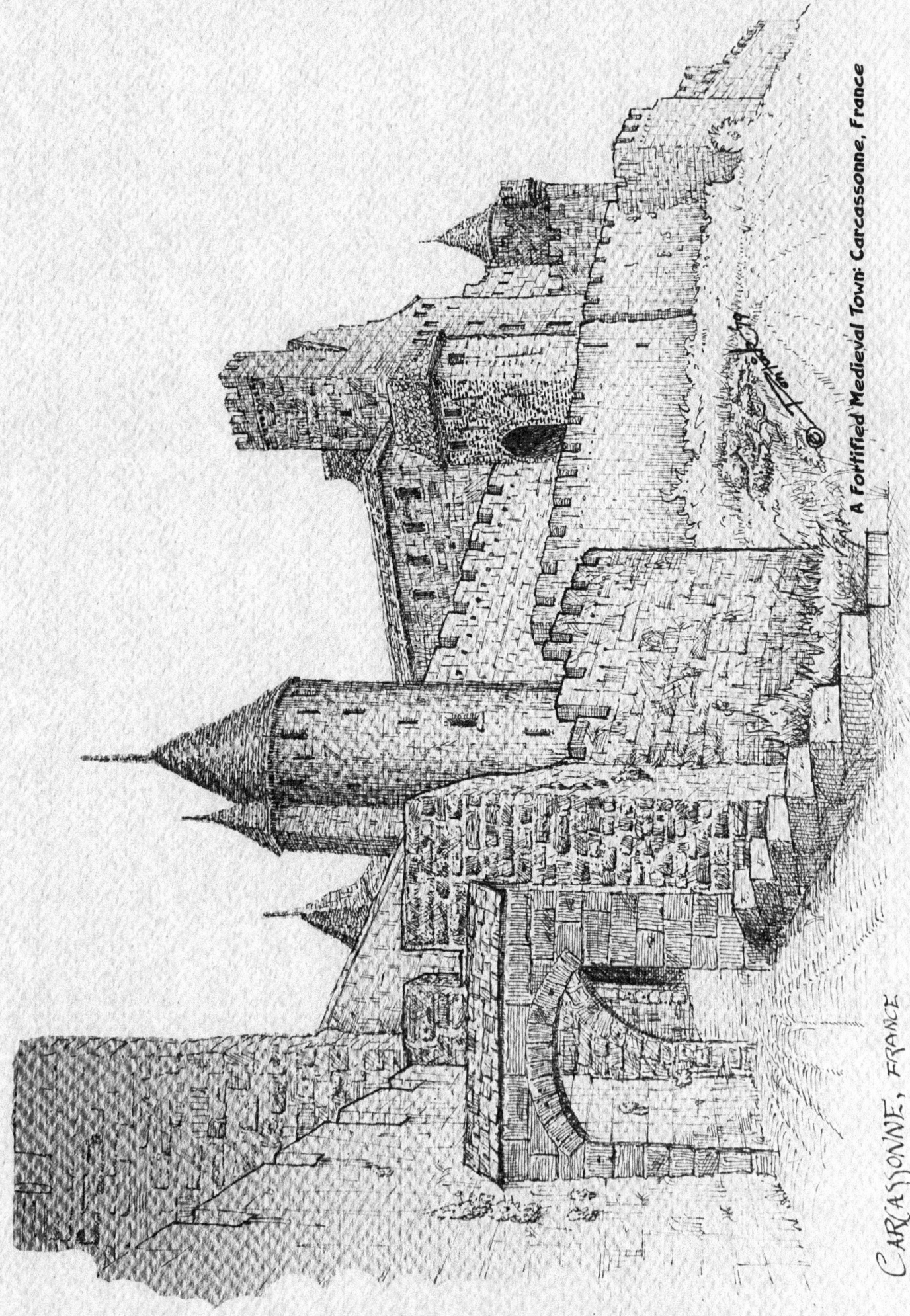

A Fortified Medieval Town: Carcassonne, France

CARCASSONNE, FRANCE

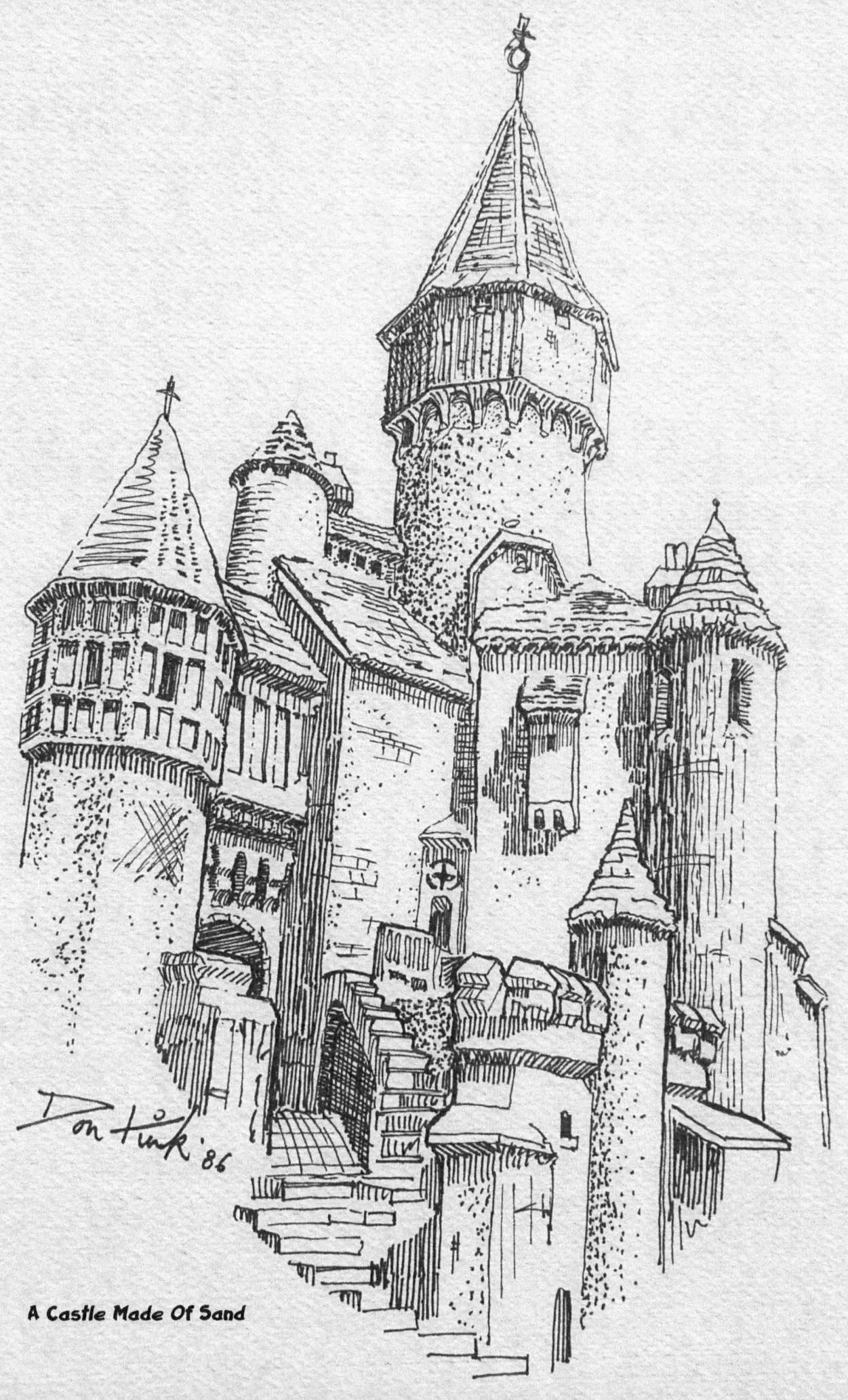

Don Tink '86

A Castle Made Of Sand

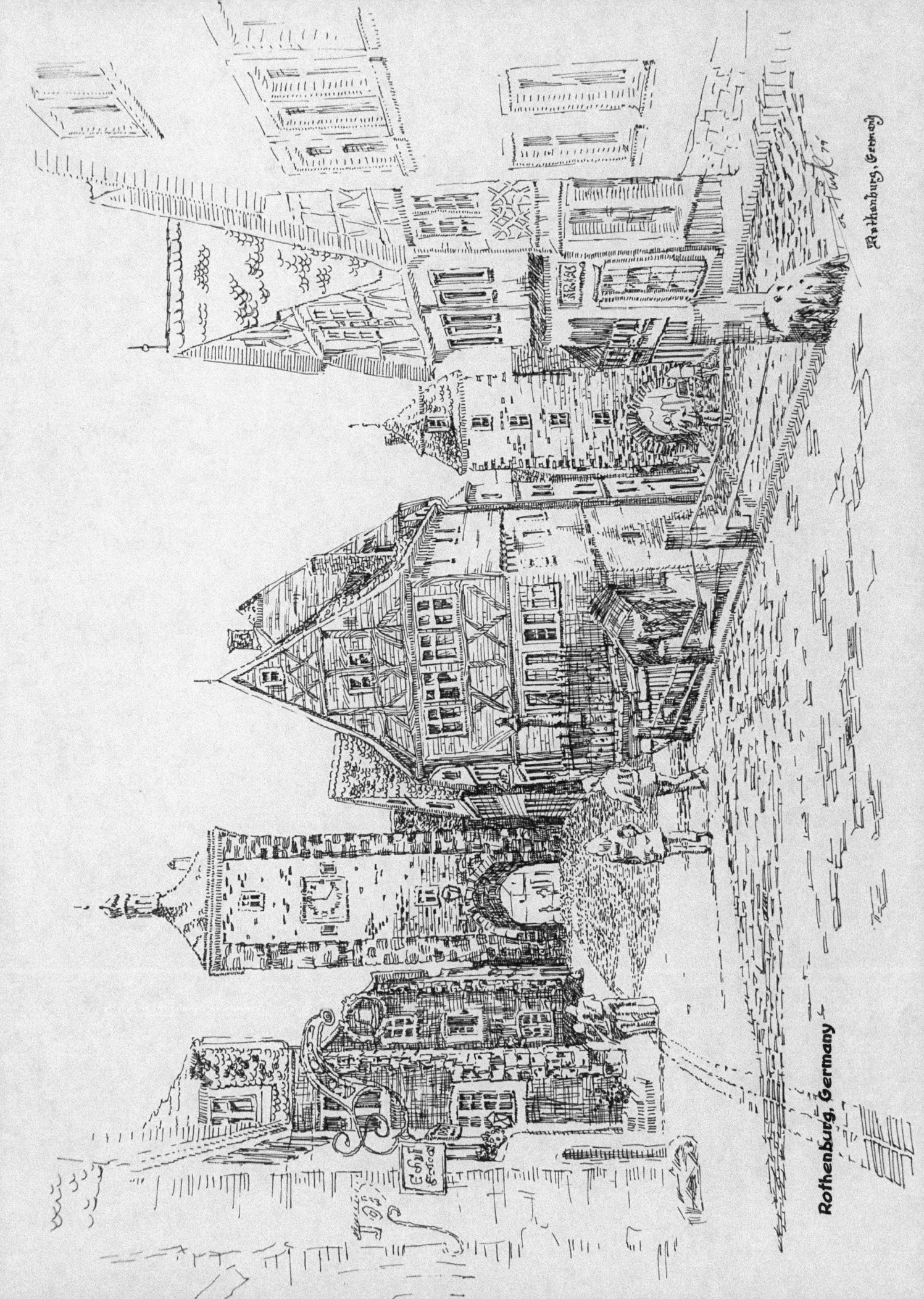

Rothenburg, Germany

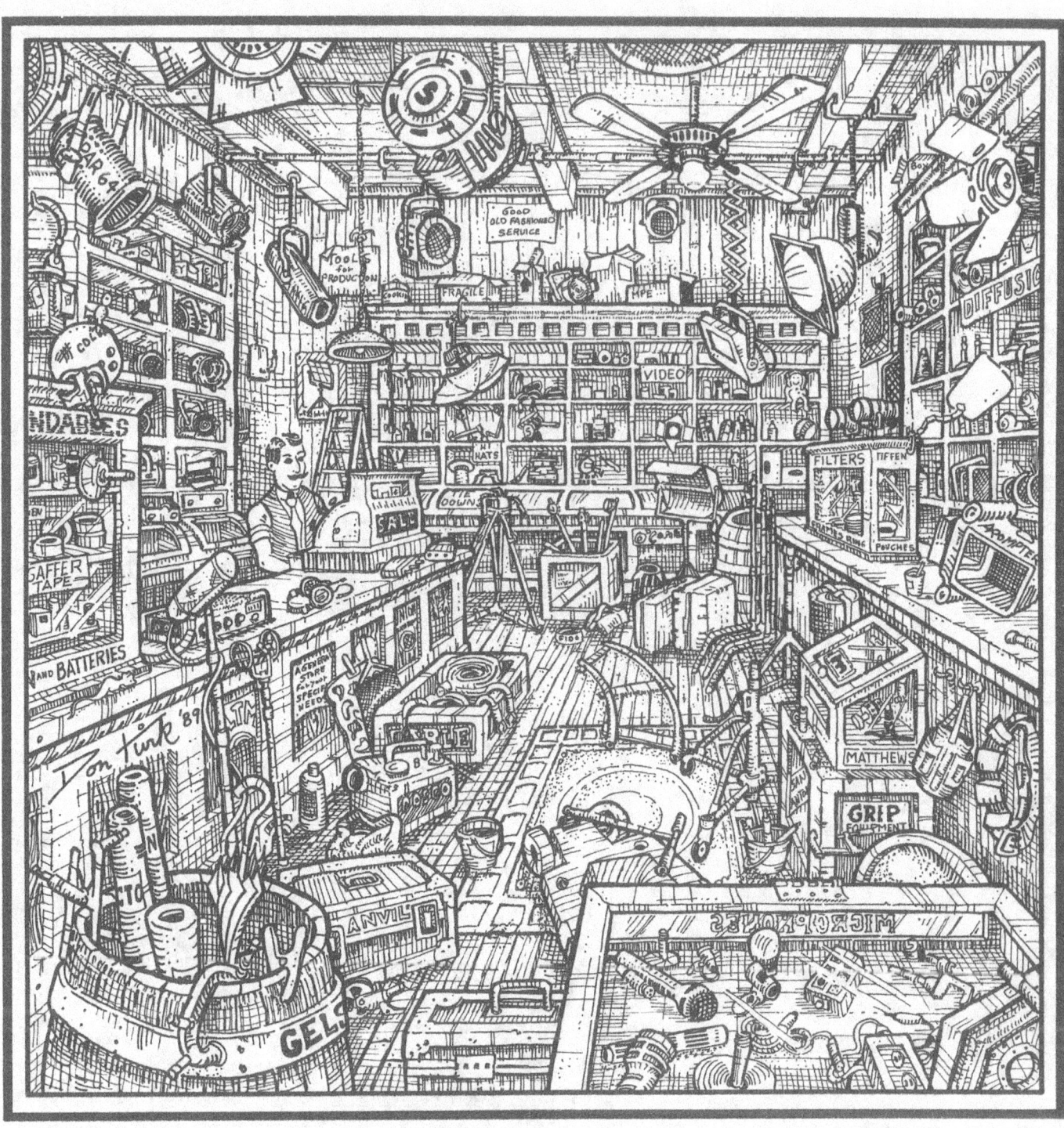

IMAGEWARE: A Motion Picture Grip And Lighting Equipment General Store

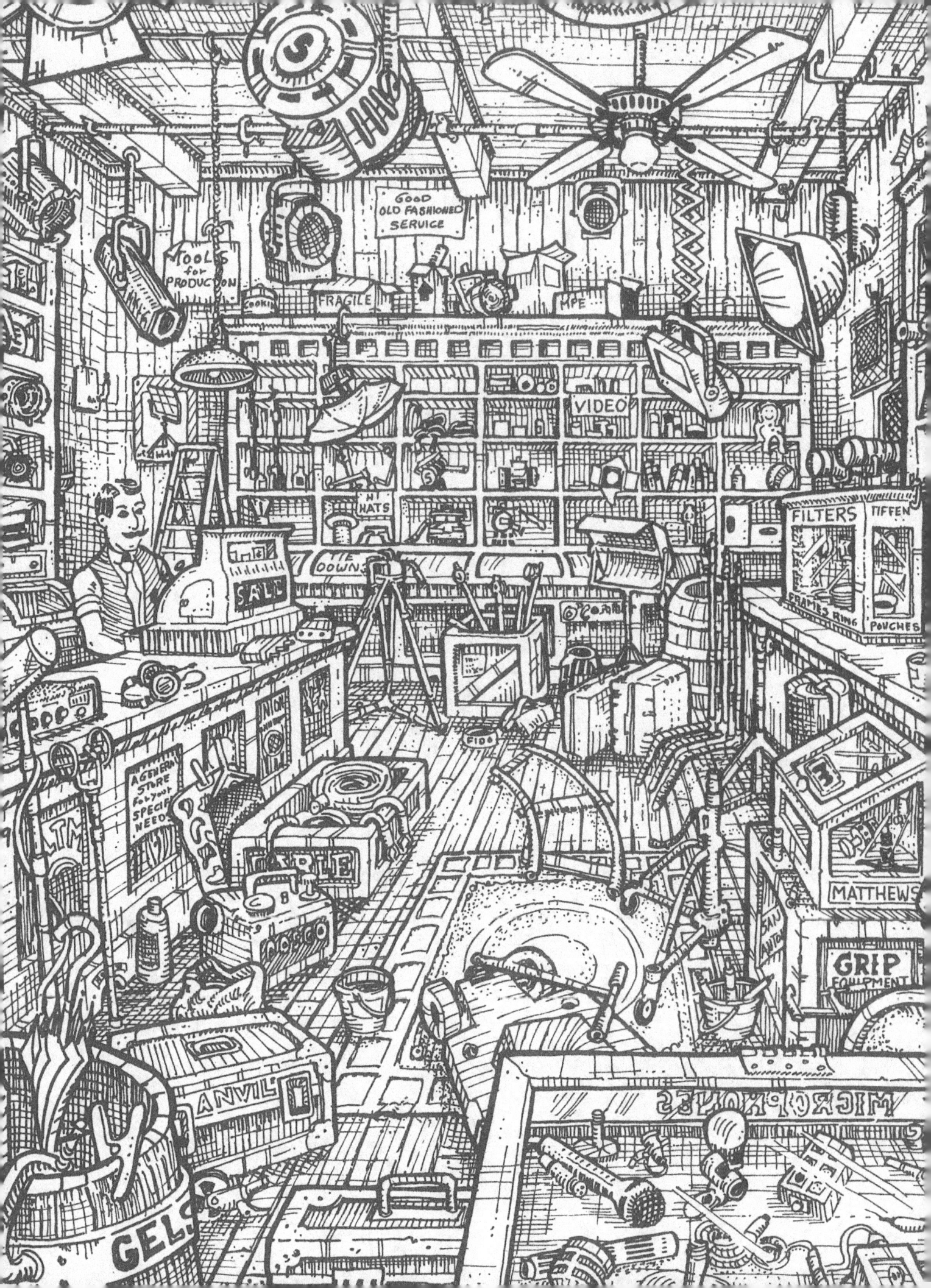

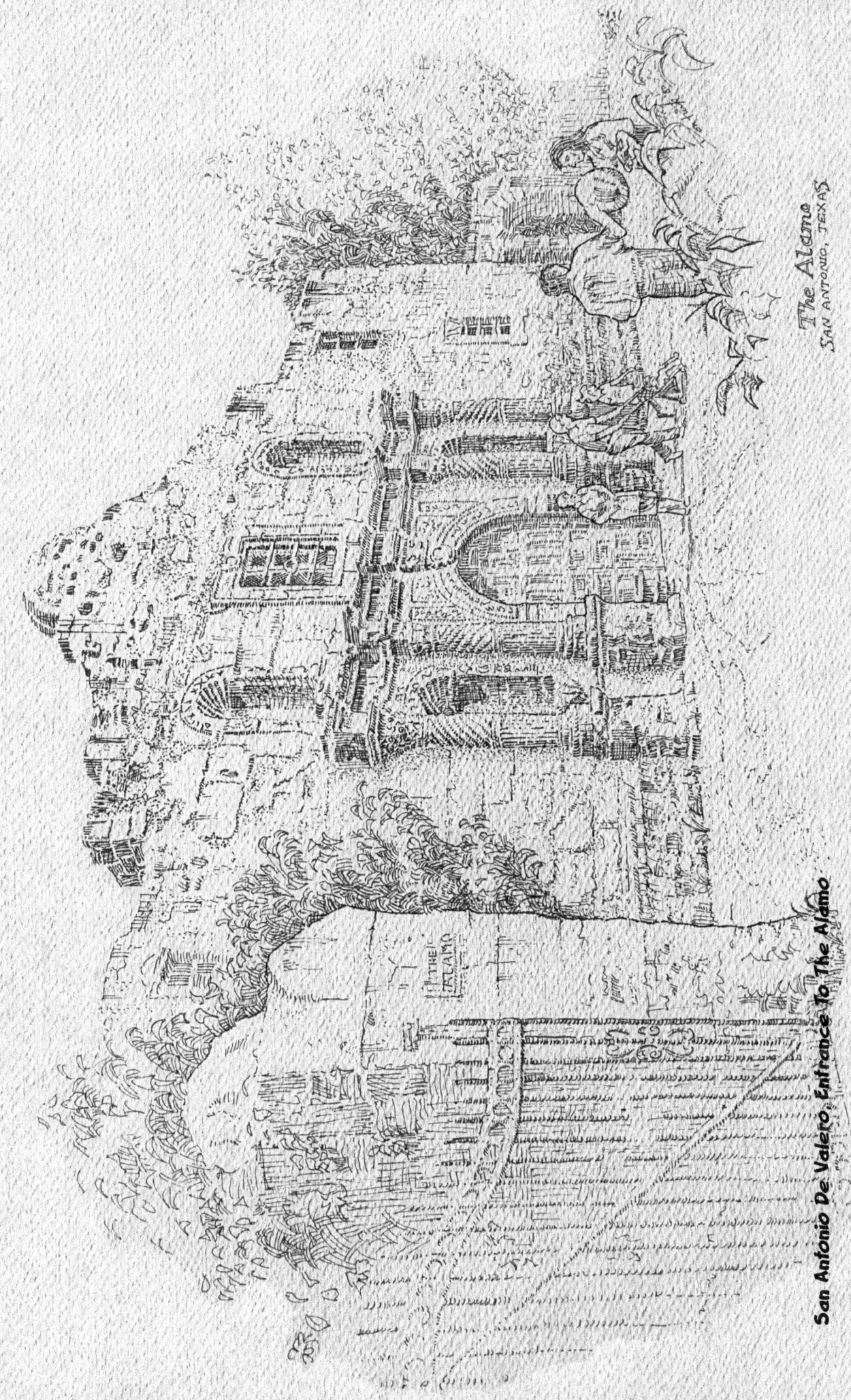

The Alamo
SAN ANTONIO, TEXAS

San Antonio De Valero, Entrance To The Alamo.

San Antonio de Valero

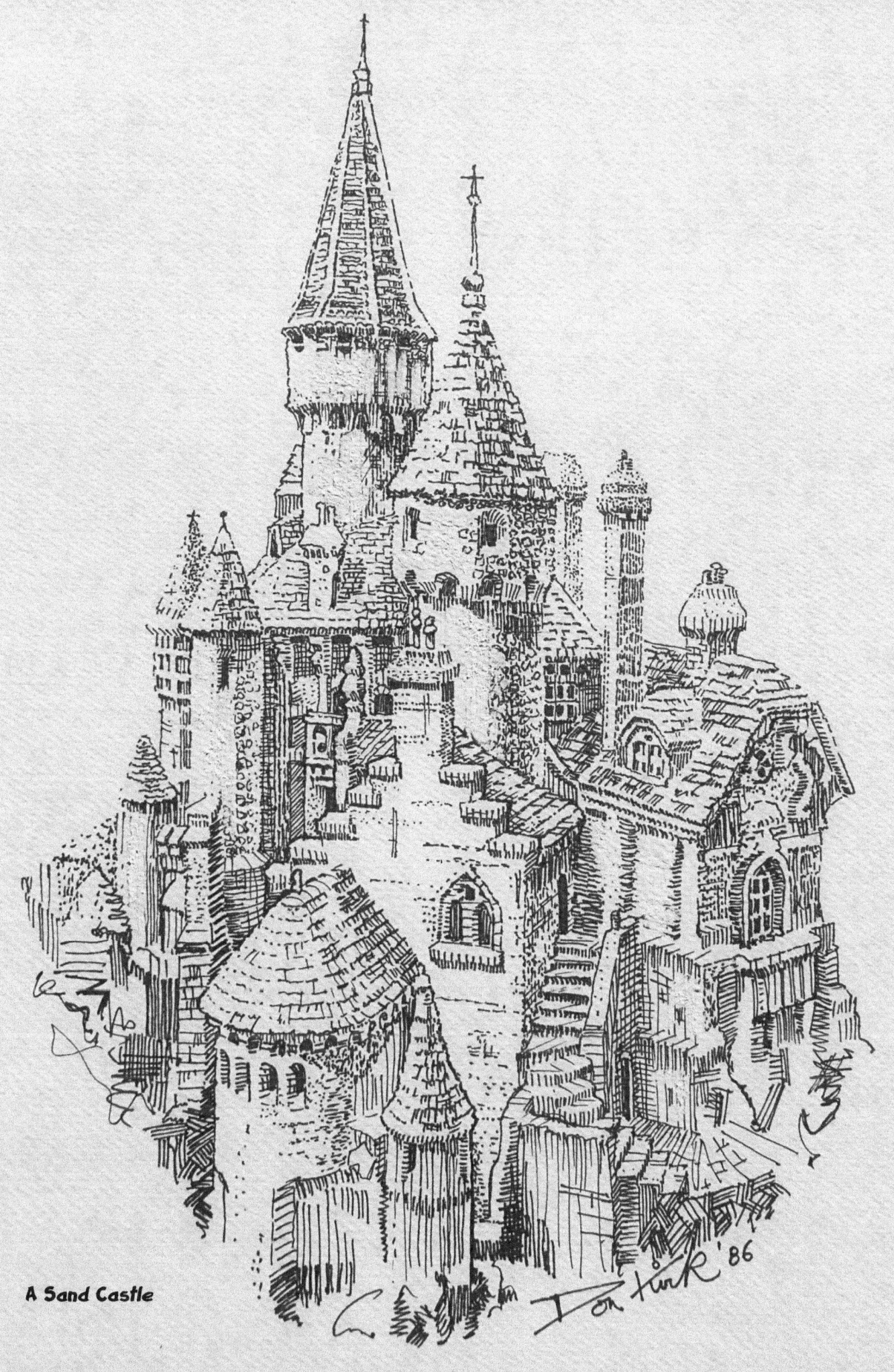

A Sand Castle

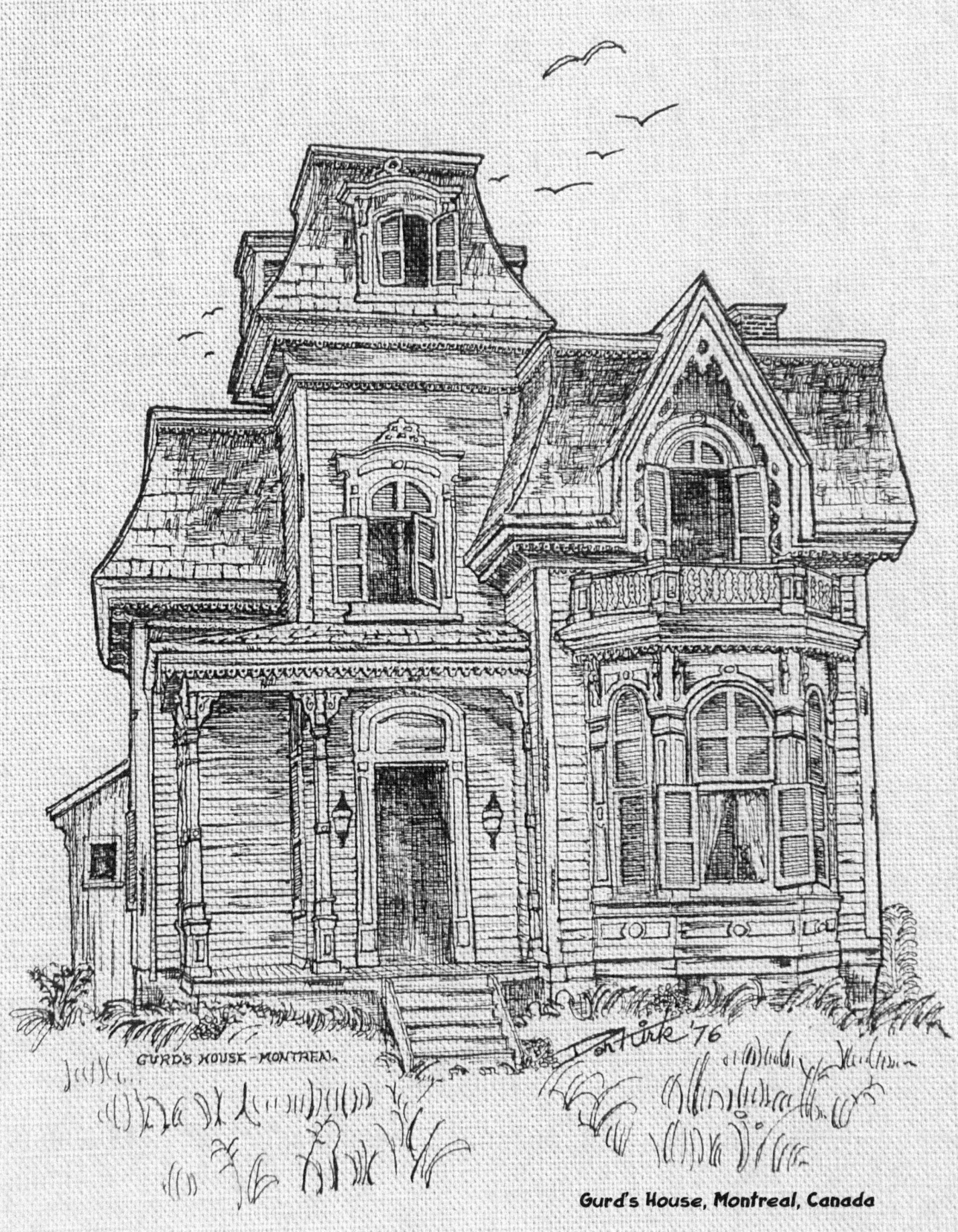

Gurd's House, Montreal, Canada

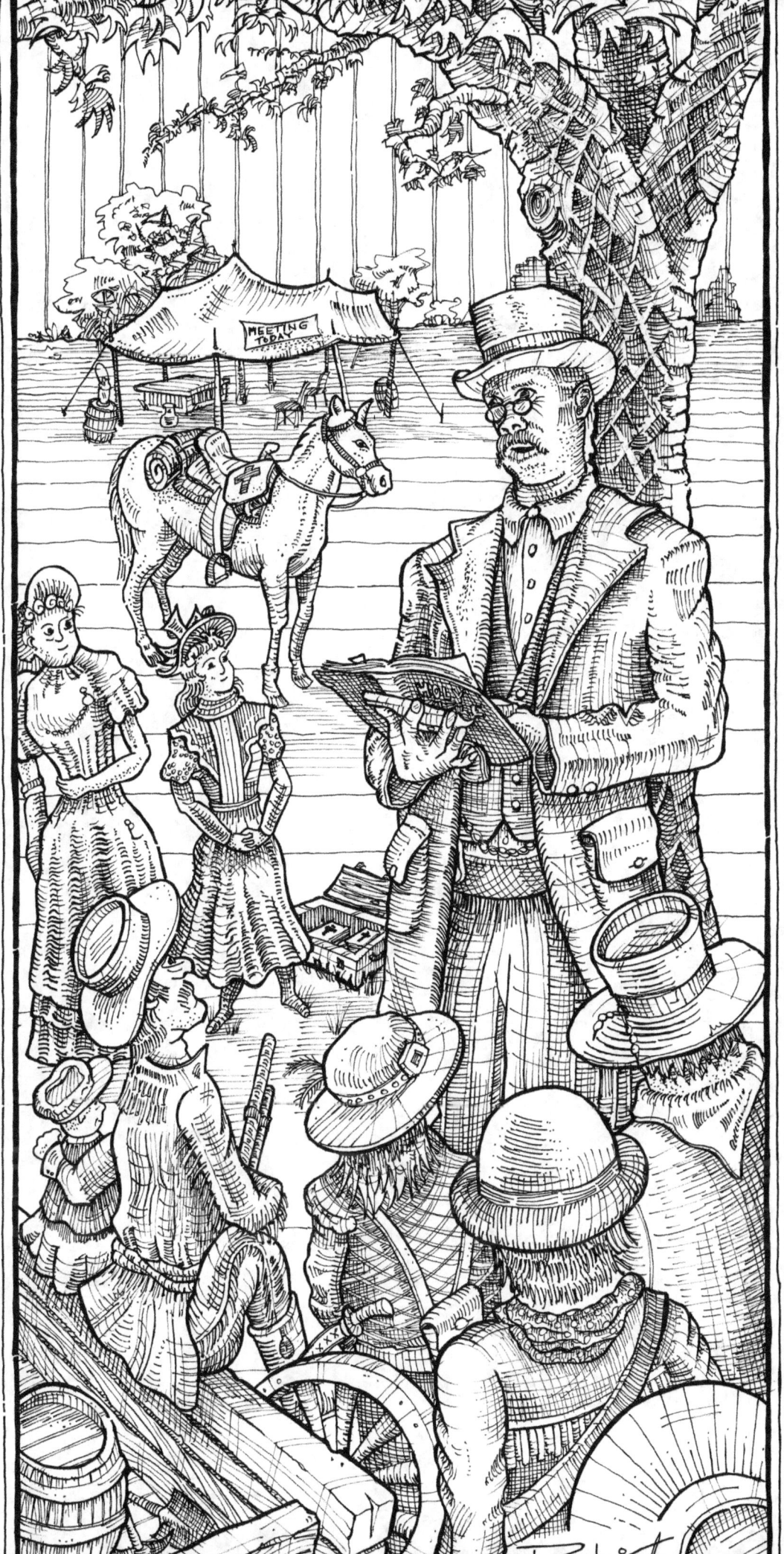

The Capitol Of Texas Park: A Circuit-Ridng Methodist Preacher In Texas, 1836

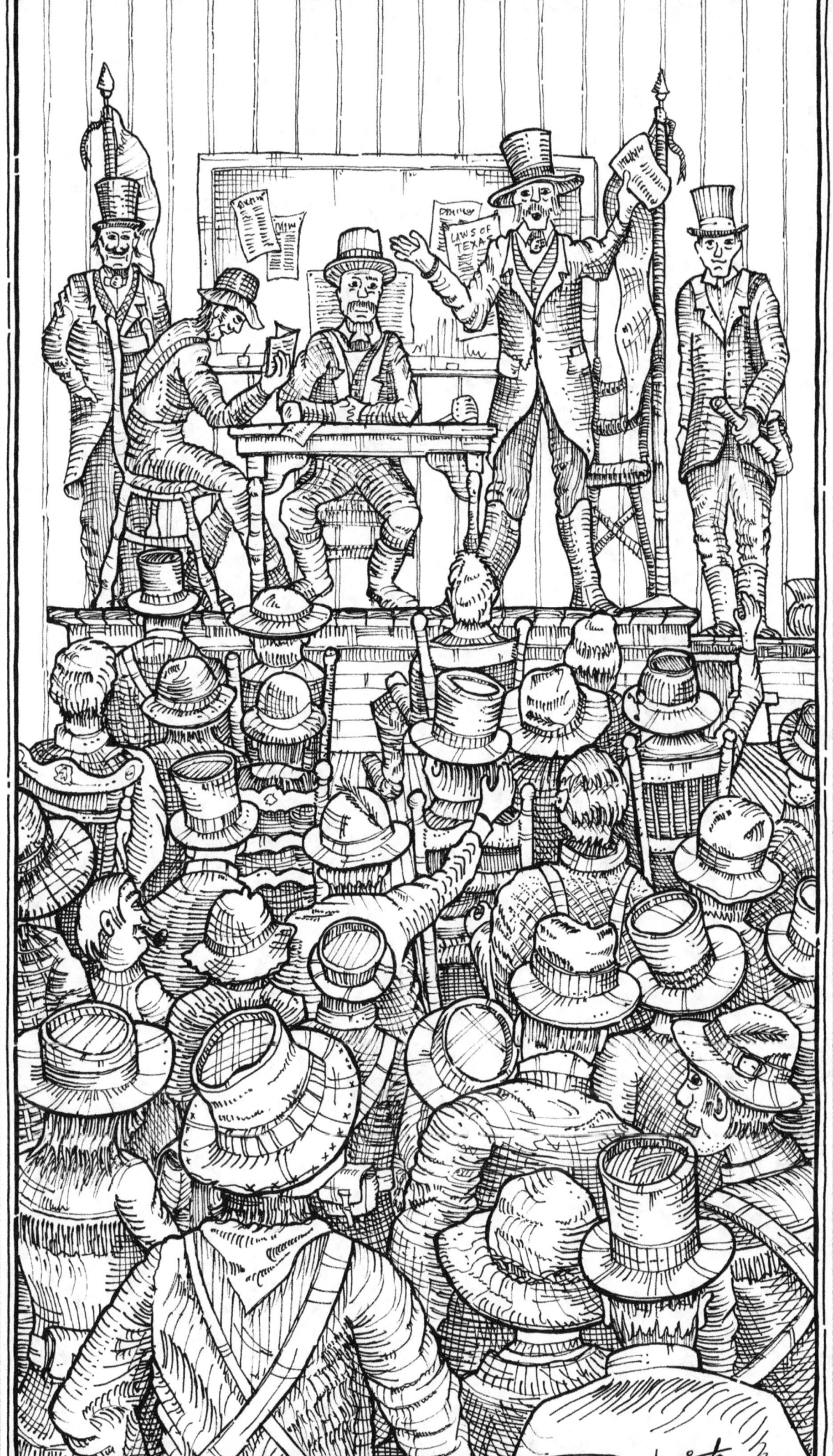

The Capitol Of Texas Park: First Senate Meeting Of The Republic Of Texas, 1836

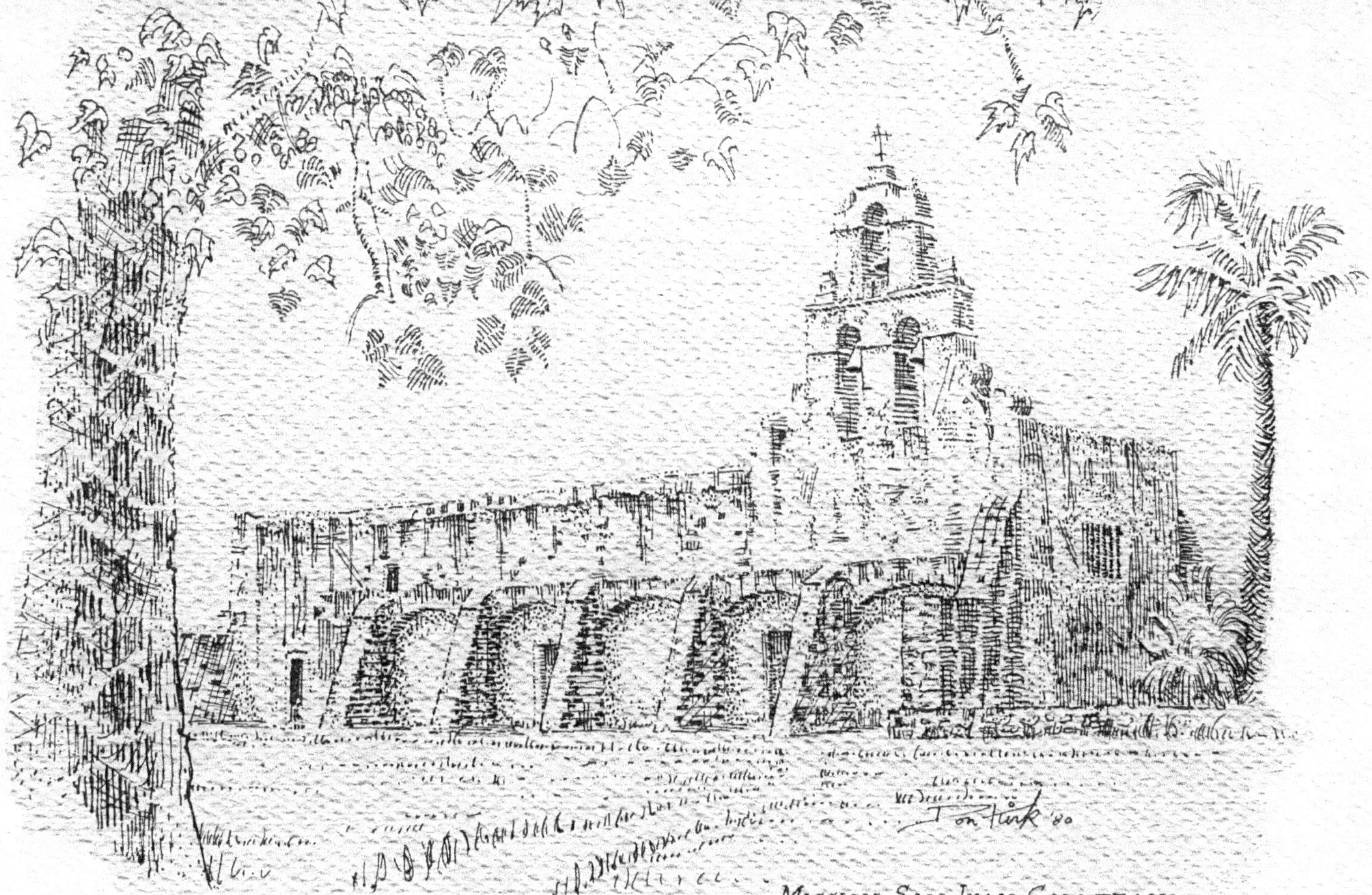

MISSION SAN JUAN CAPISTRANO

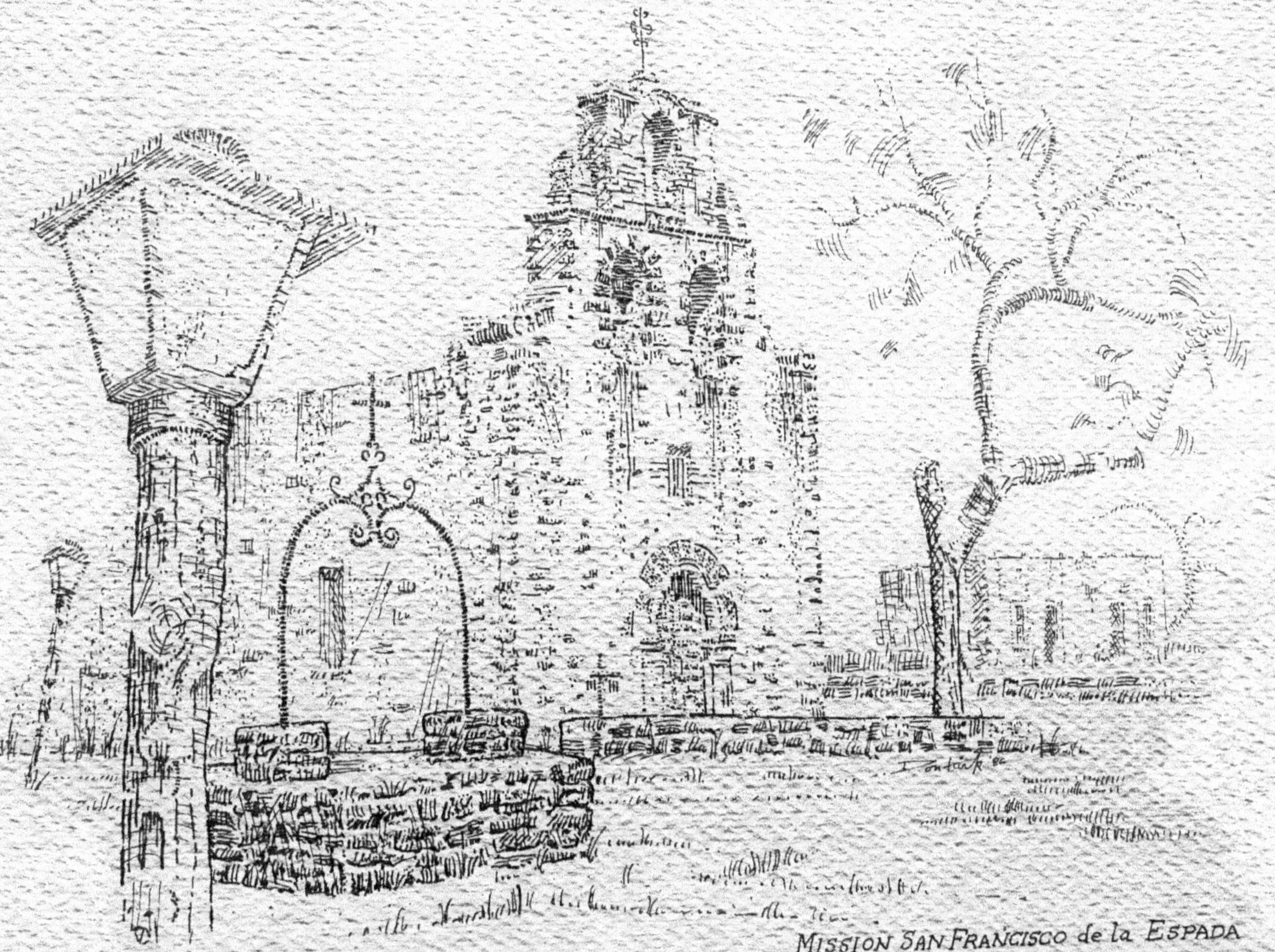

MISSION SAN FRANCISCO de la ESPADA

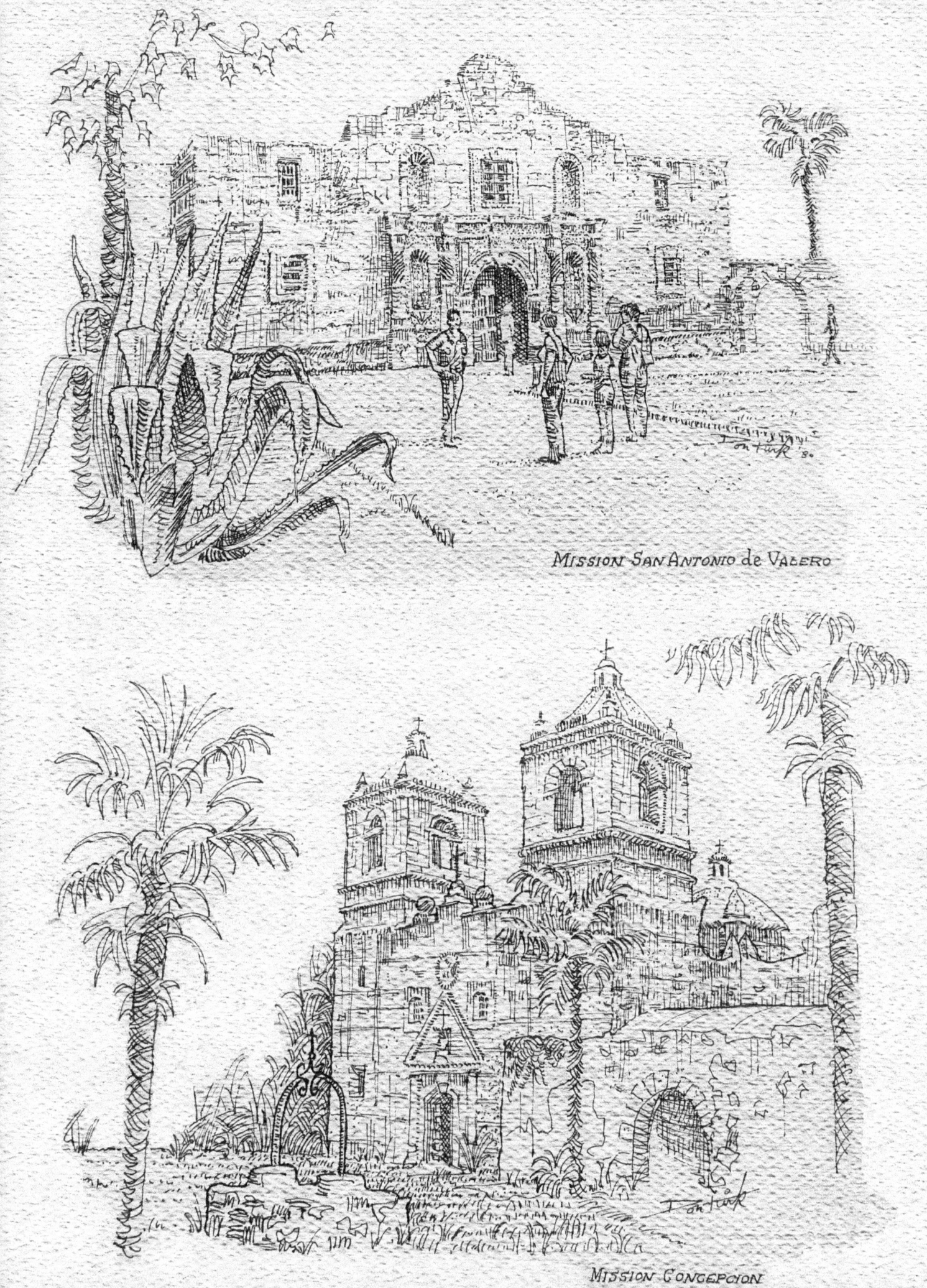

Mission San Antonio de Valero

Mission Concepcion

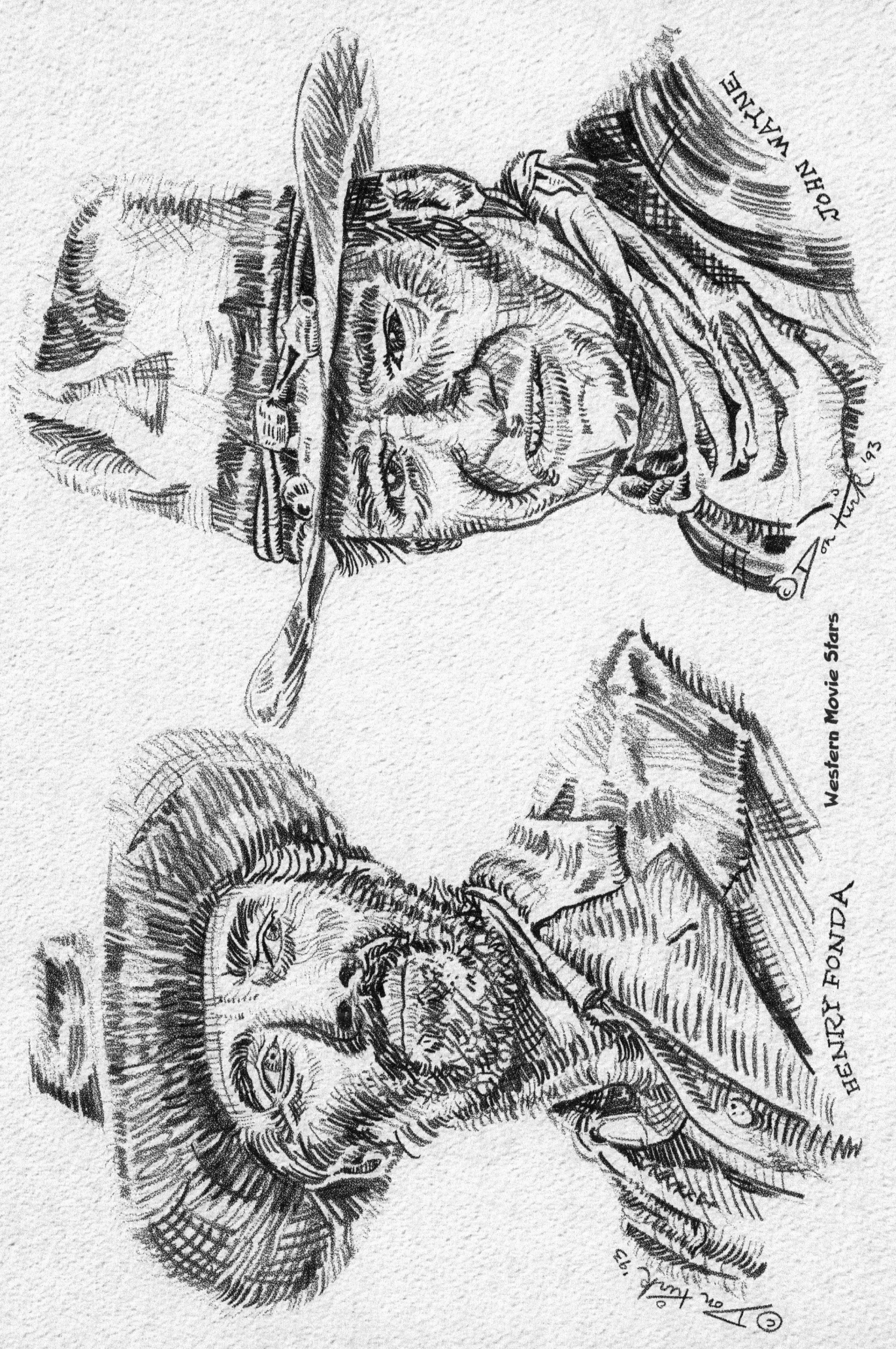

JOHN WAYNE

Western Movie Stars

HENRY FONDA

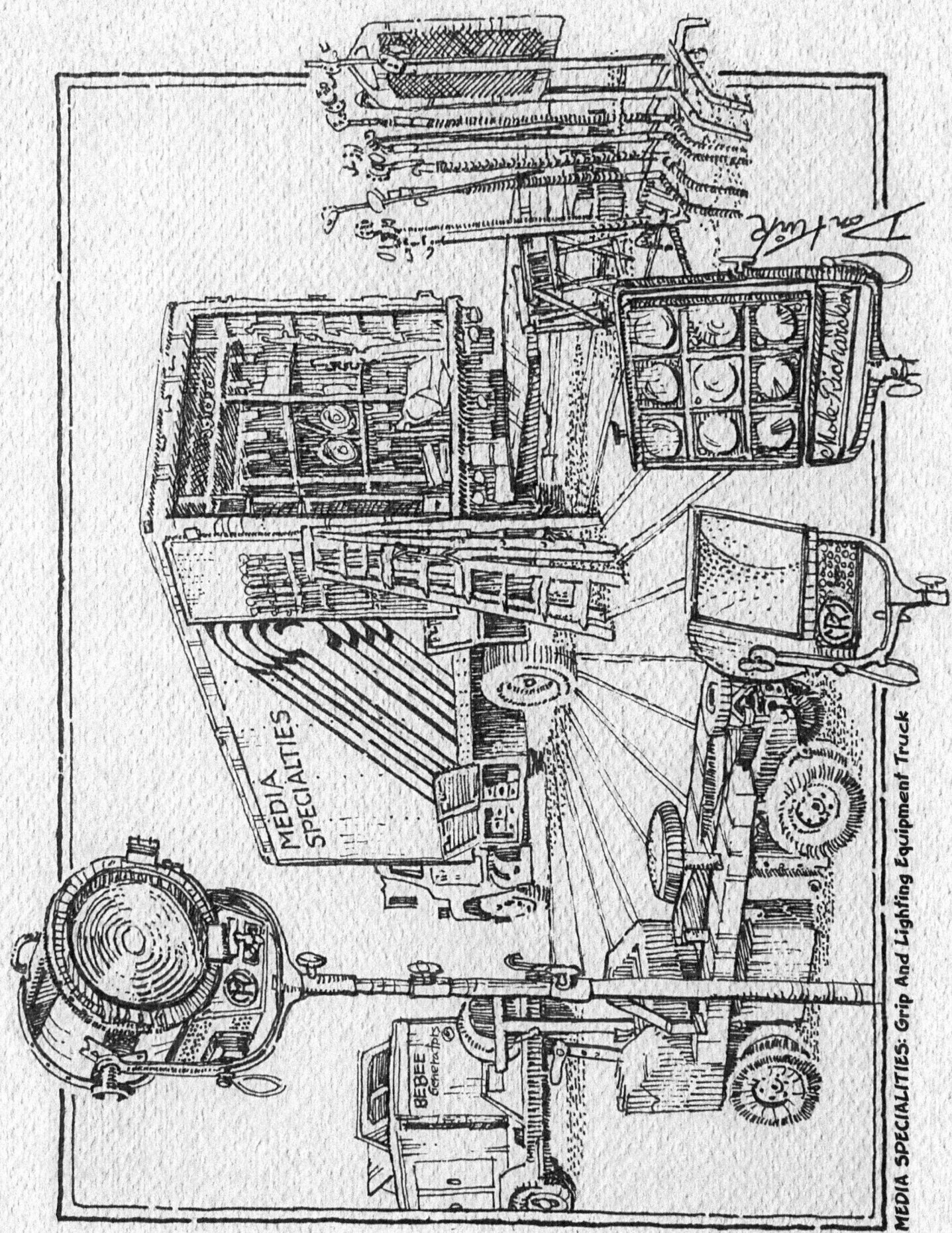

MEDIA SPECIALTIES: Grip And Lighting Equipment Truck

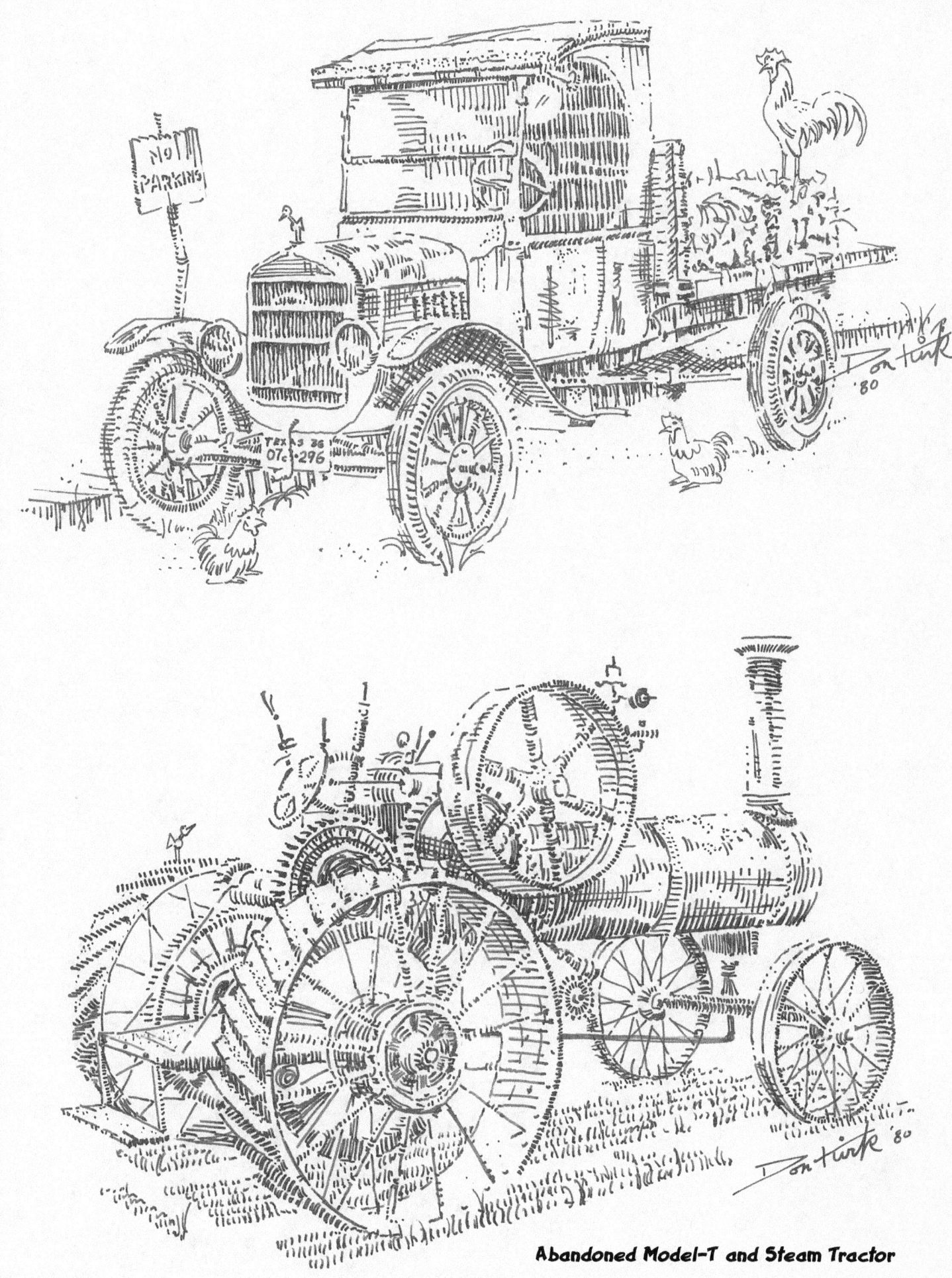

Abandoned Model-T and Steam Tractor

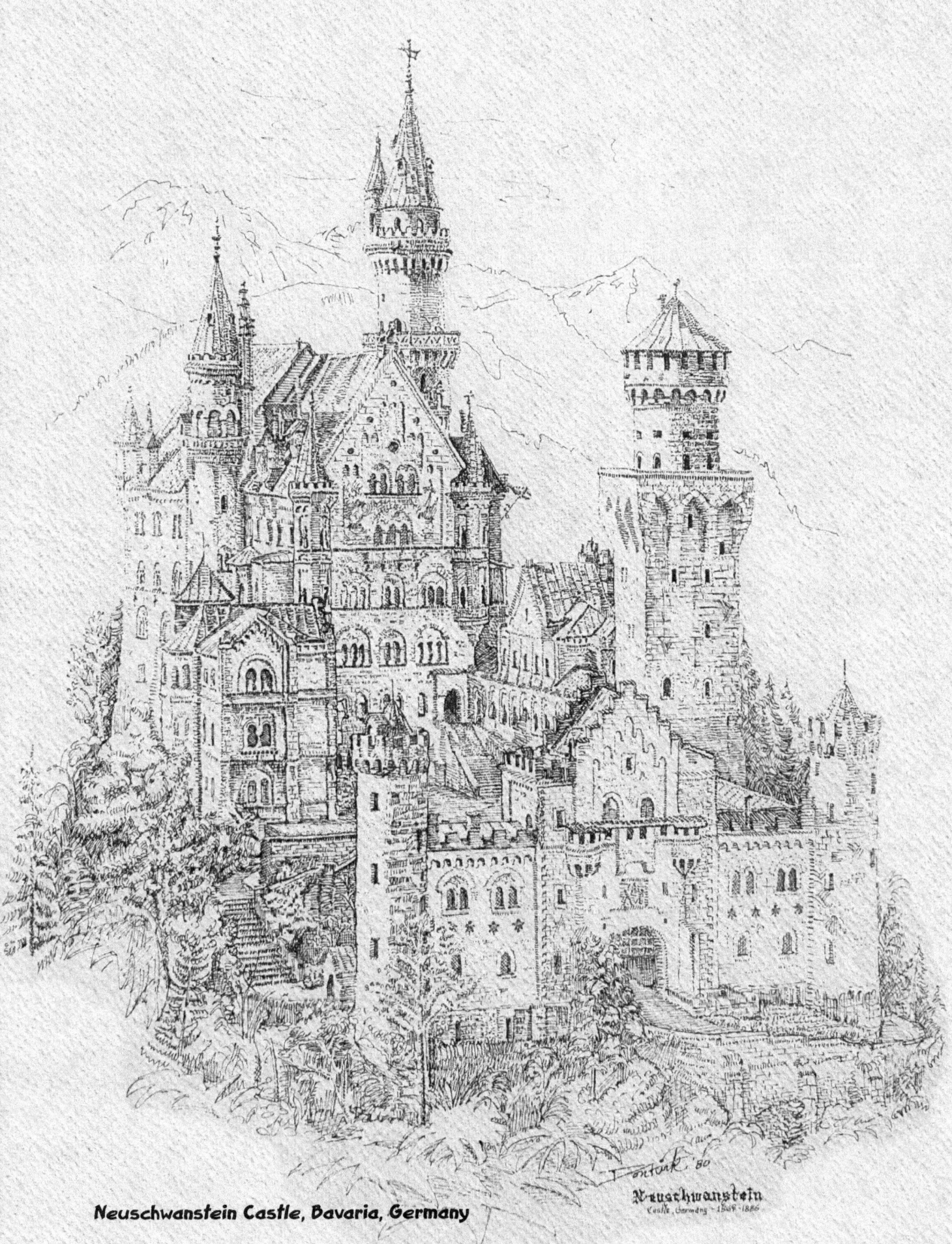

Neuschwanstein Castle, Bavaria, Germany

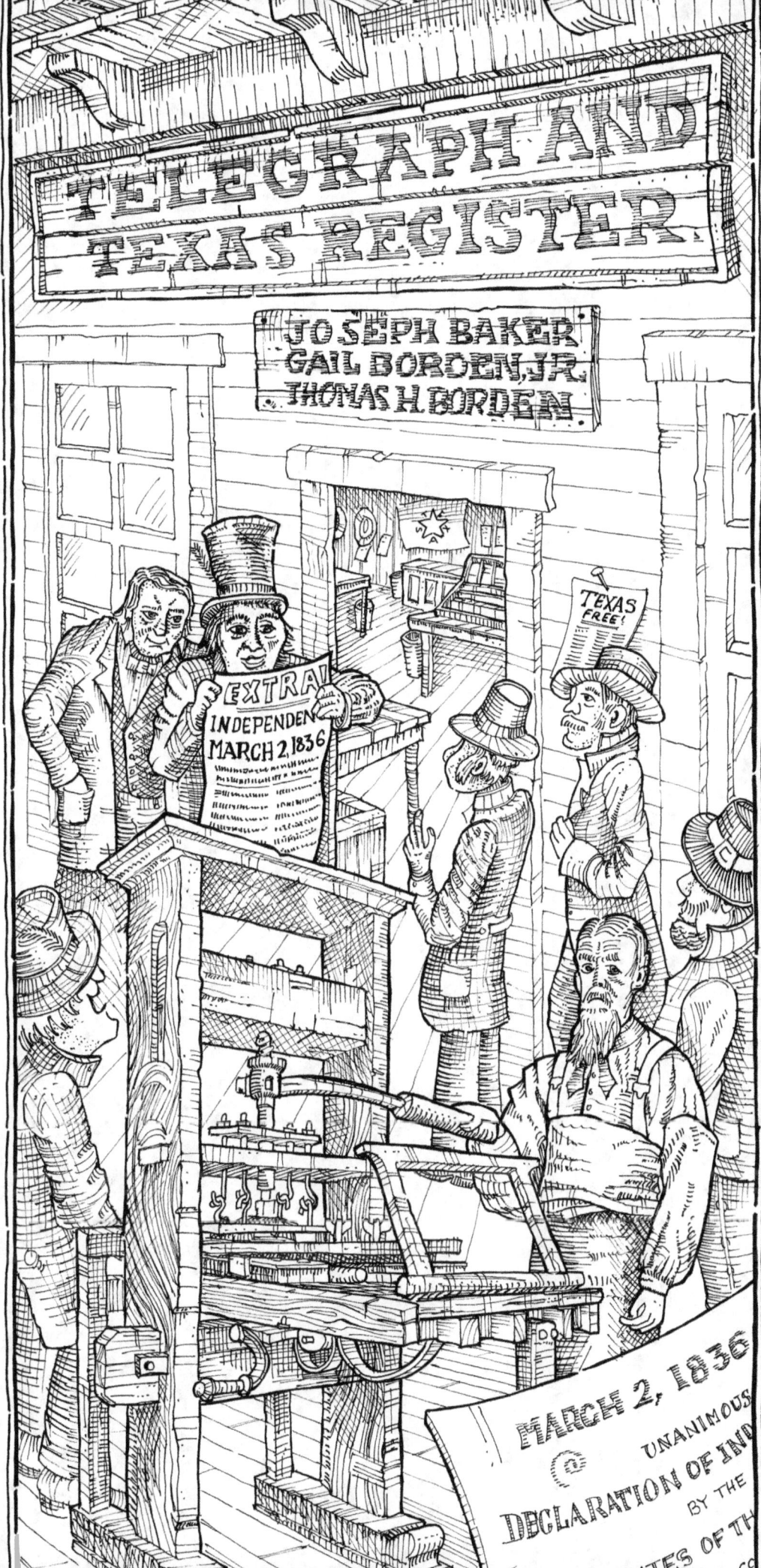

The Capitol Of Texas Park: Telegraph And Texas Register, Columbia, 1836

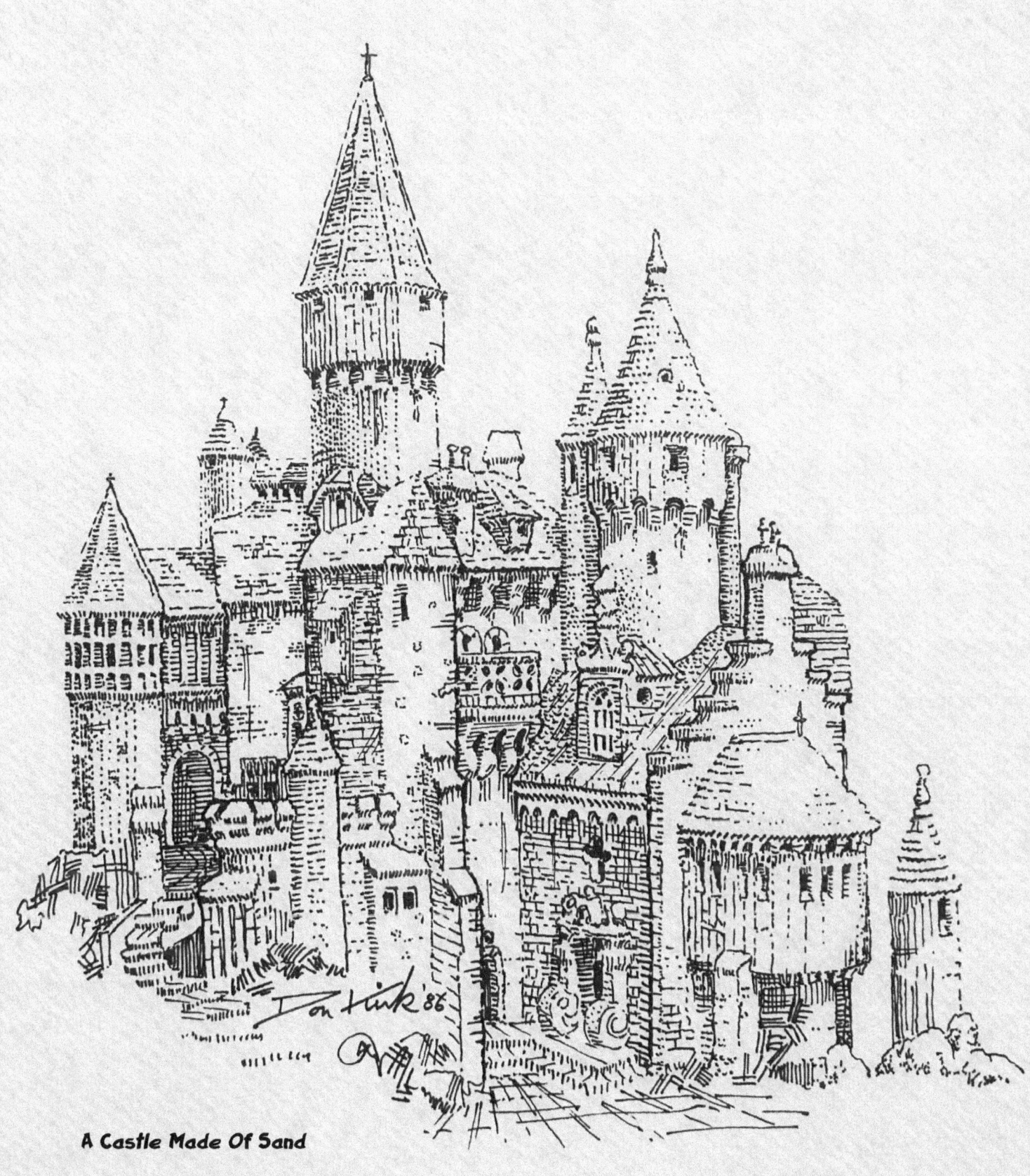

A Castle Made Of Sand

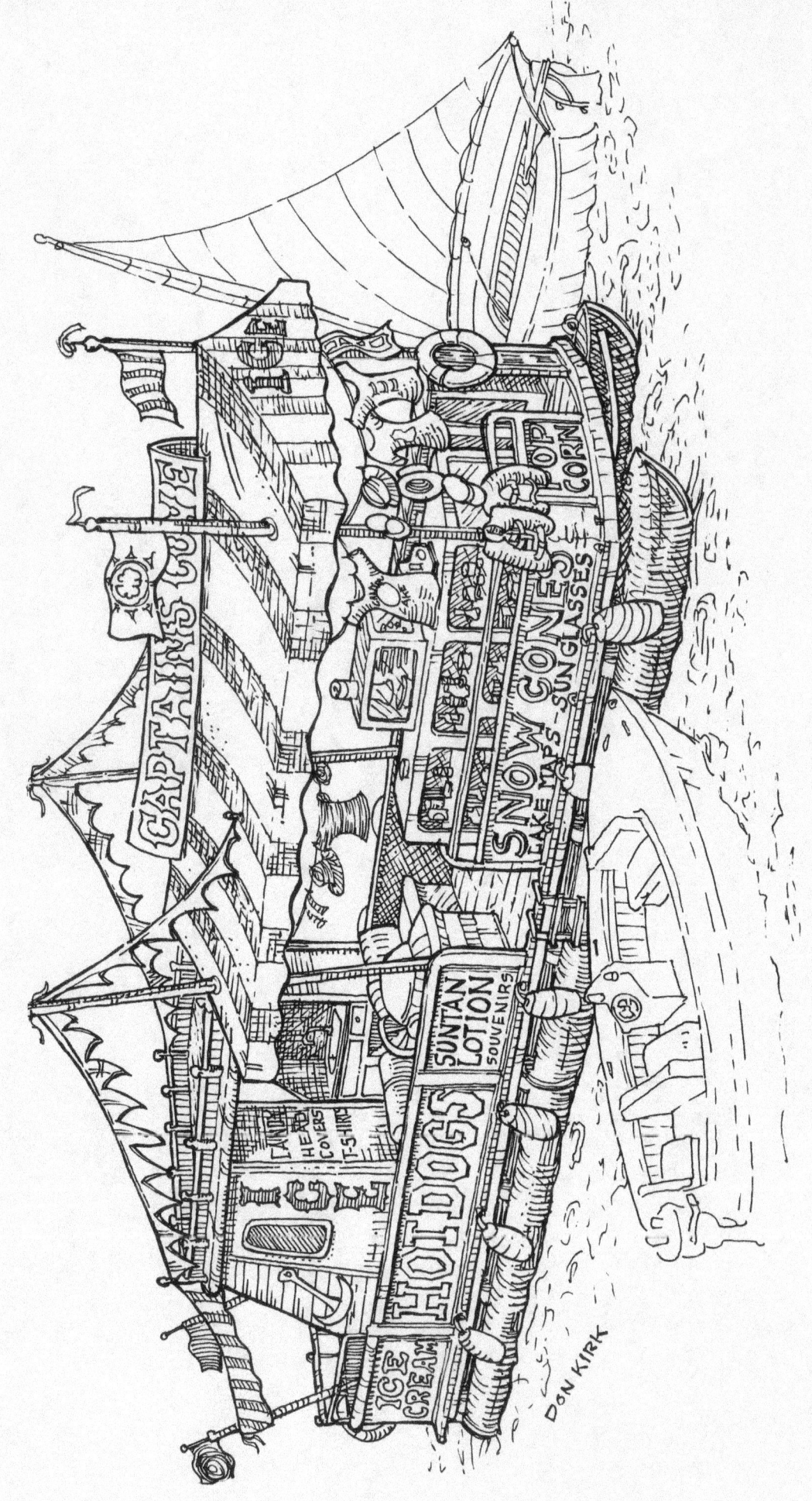

Canyon Lake, Texas, Hotdog Stand On A Pontoon Boat

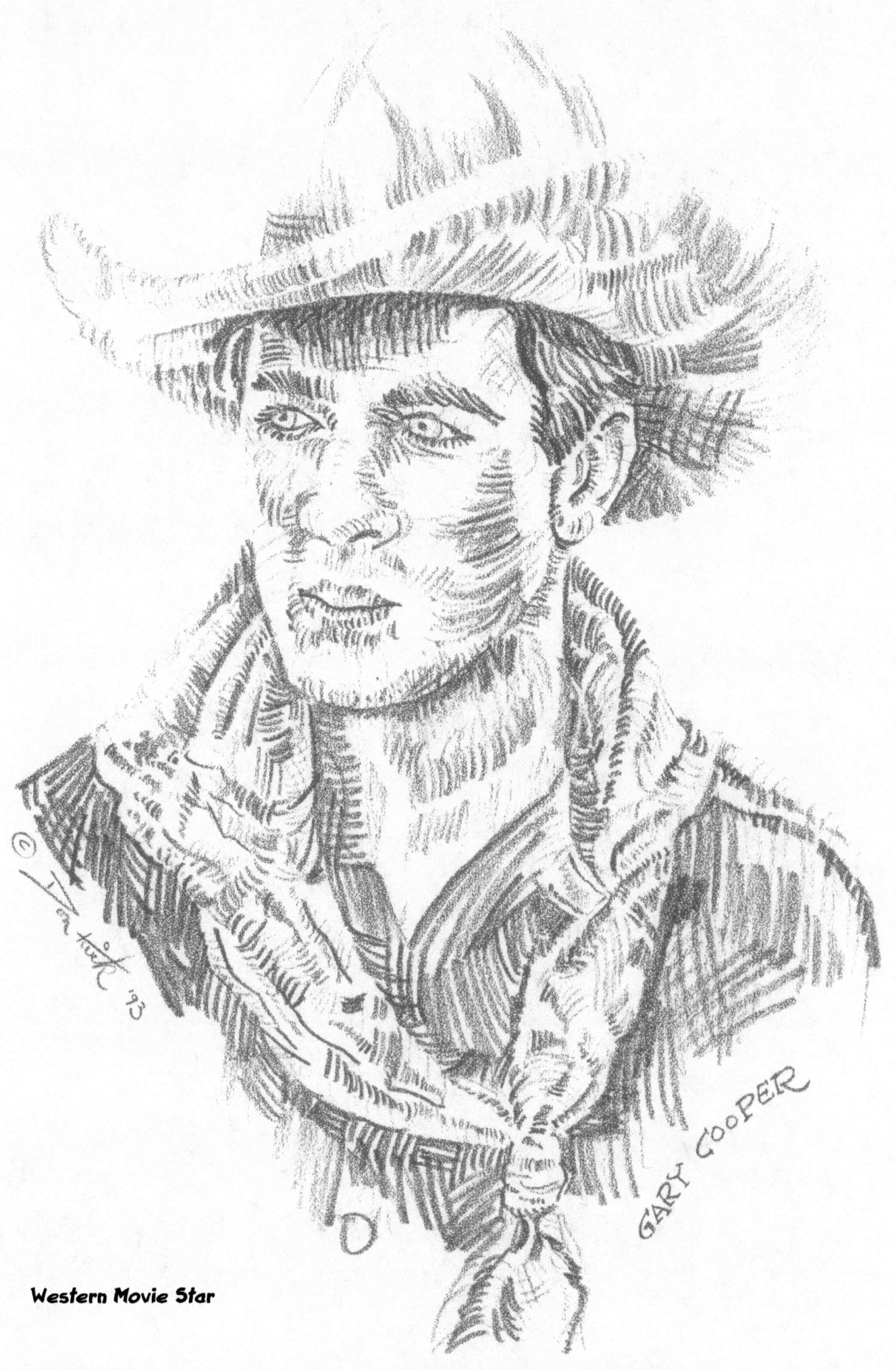

GARY COOPER

Western Movie Star

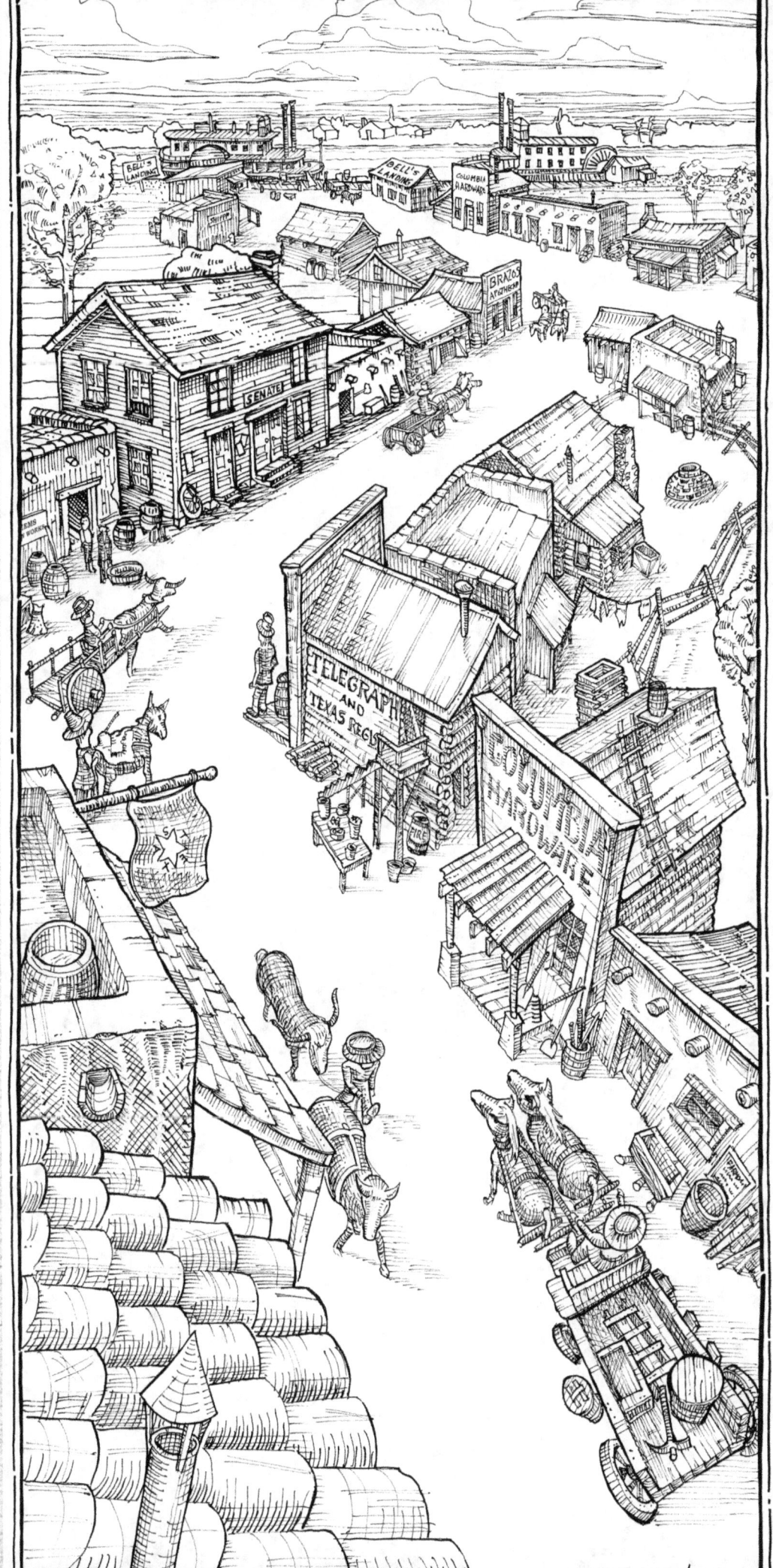

The Capitol Of Texas Park: The Town Of Columbia, Texas In 1836

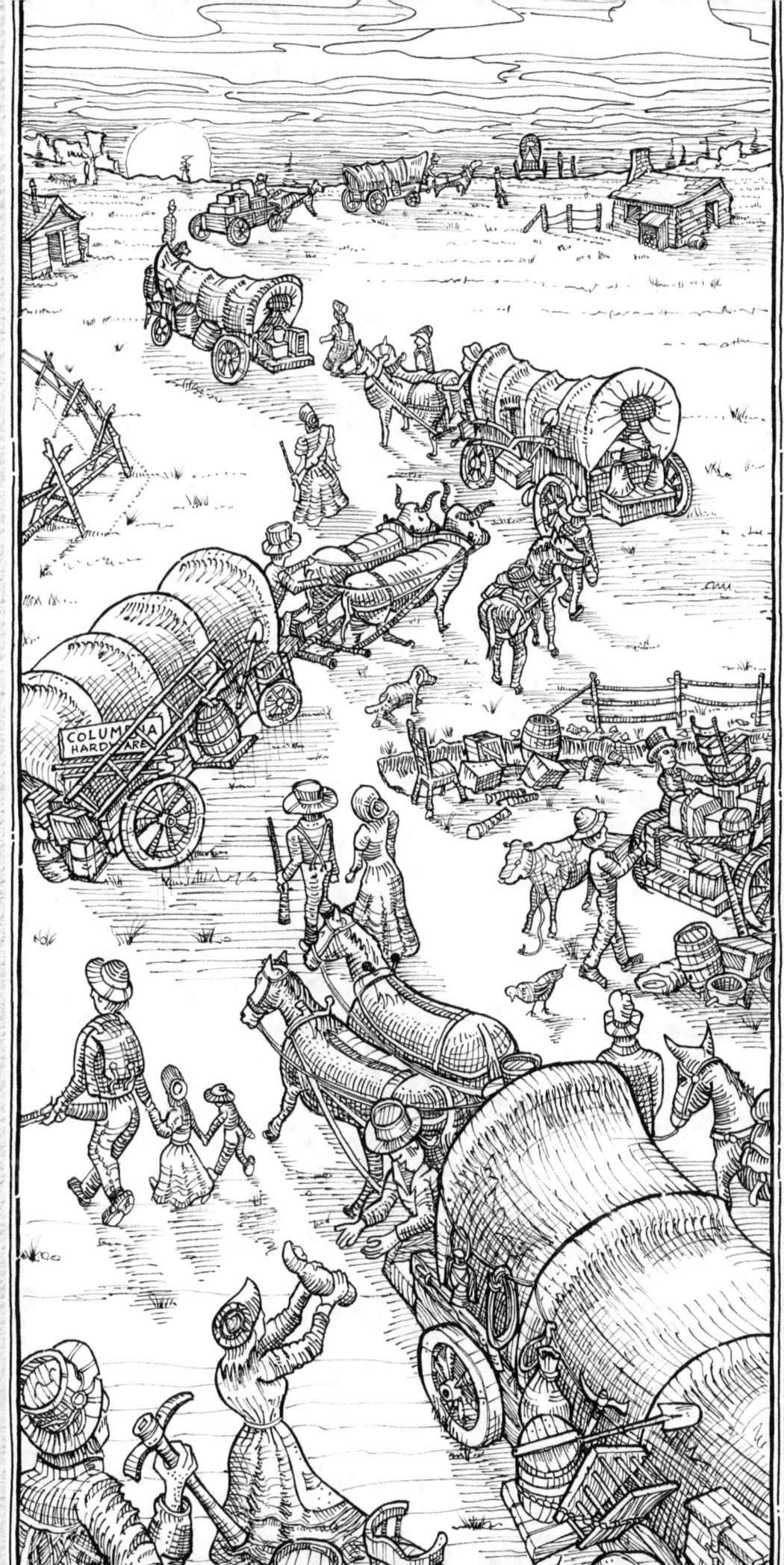

The Capitol Of Texas Park: Entire Families Leaving Columbia, Texas, Fleeing From General Santa Anna In 1836

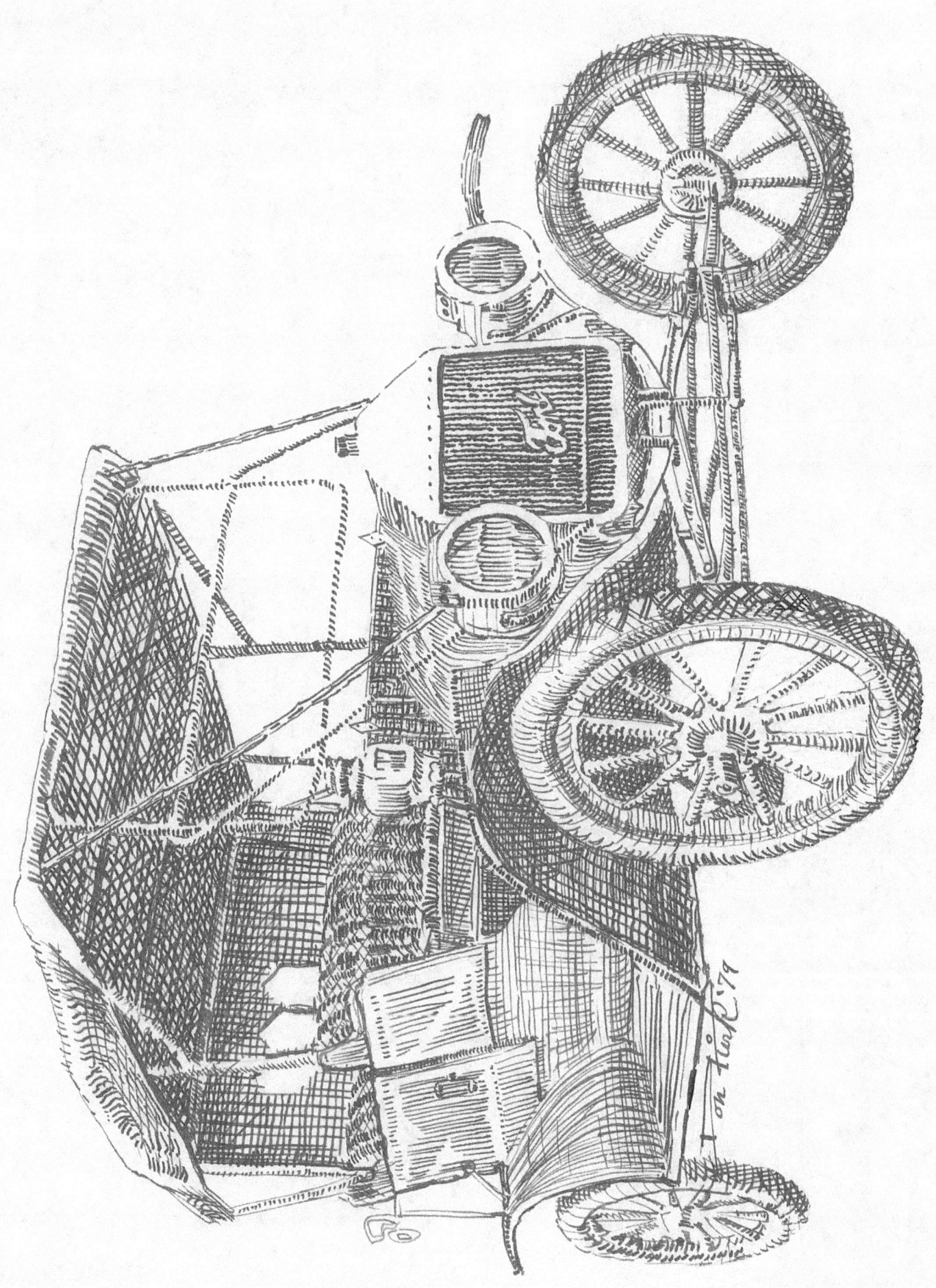

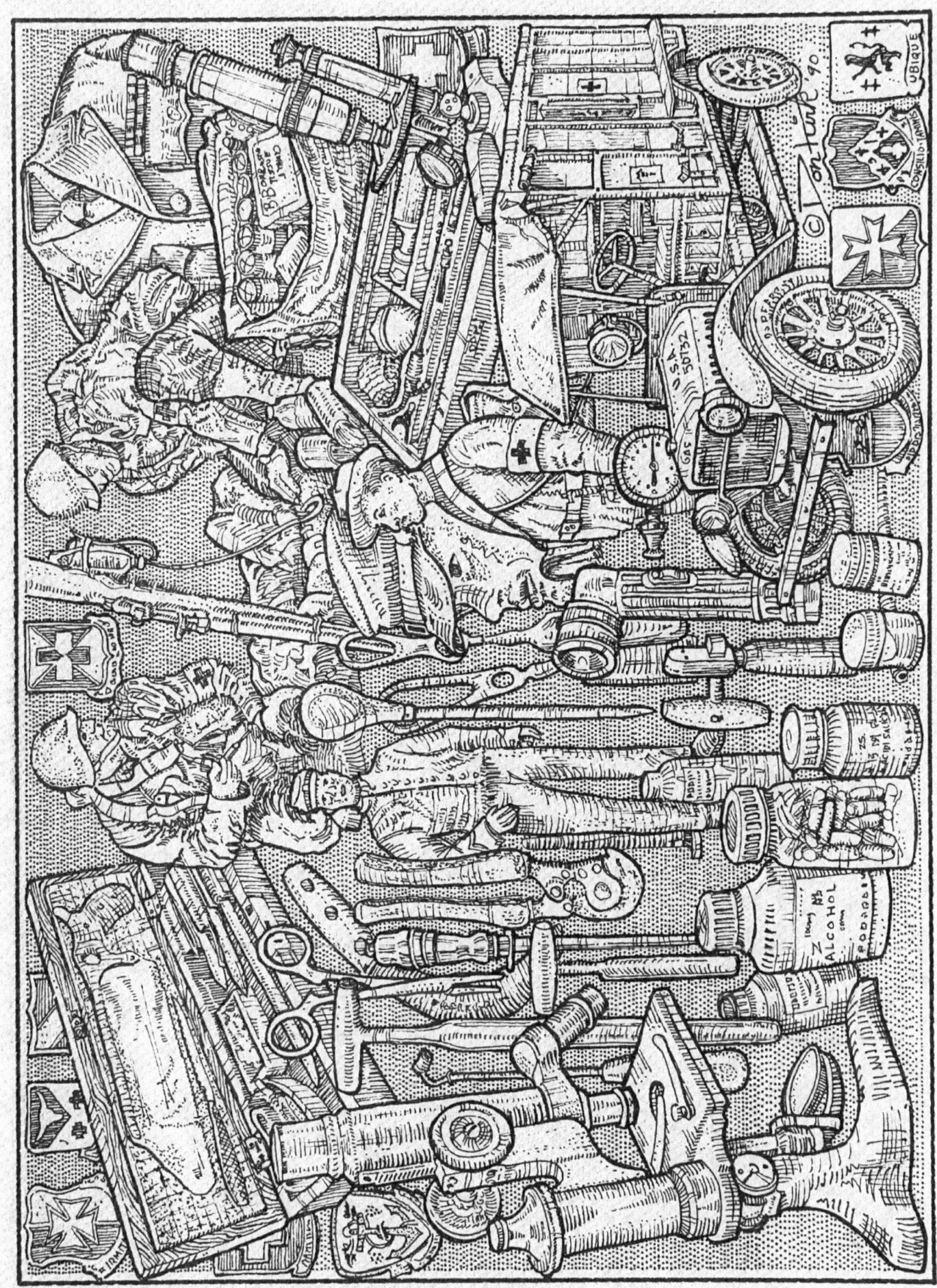

United States Army Medical Department Museum Artifacts

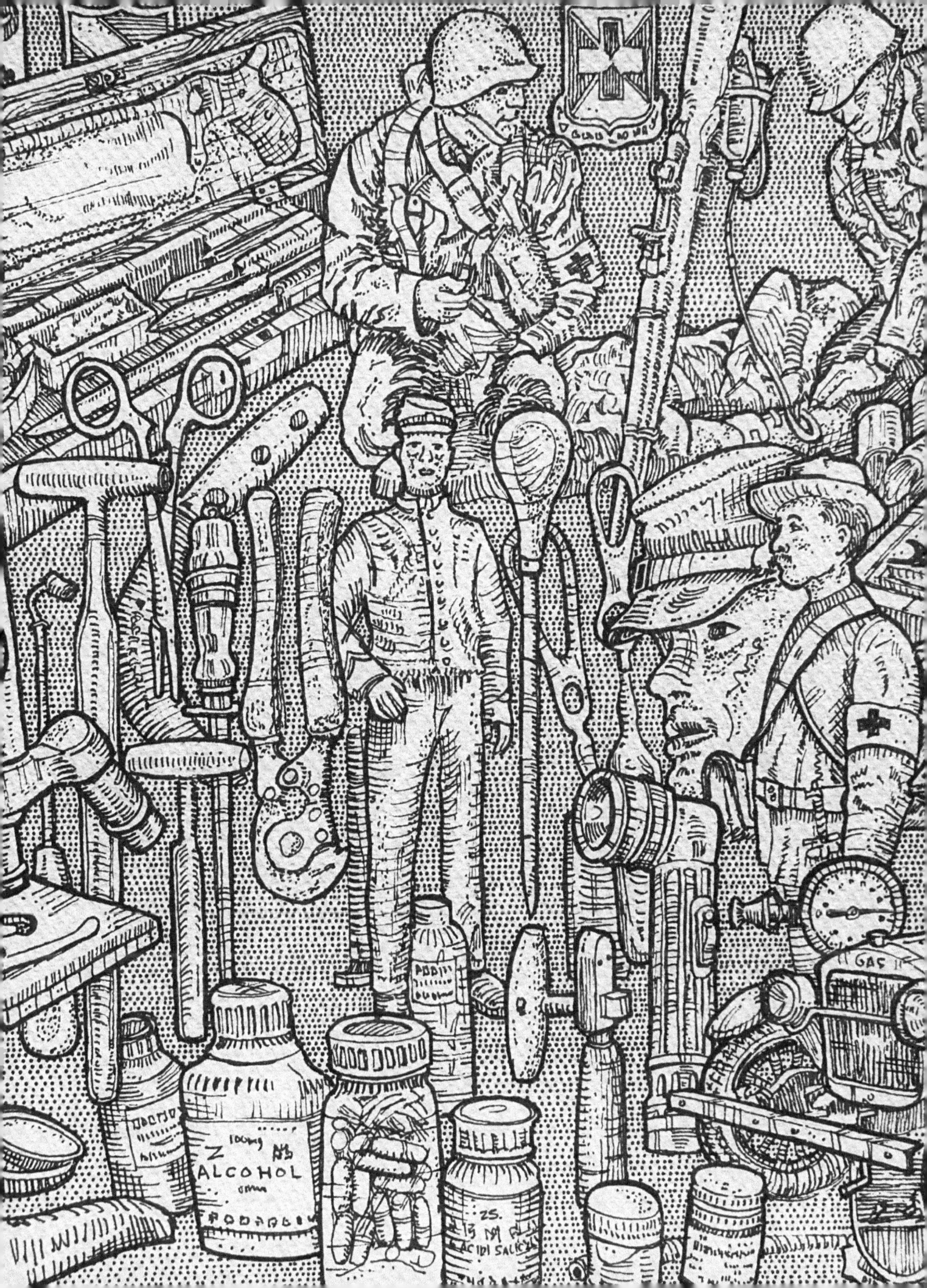

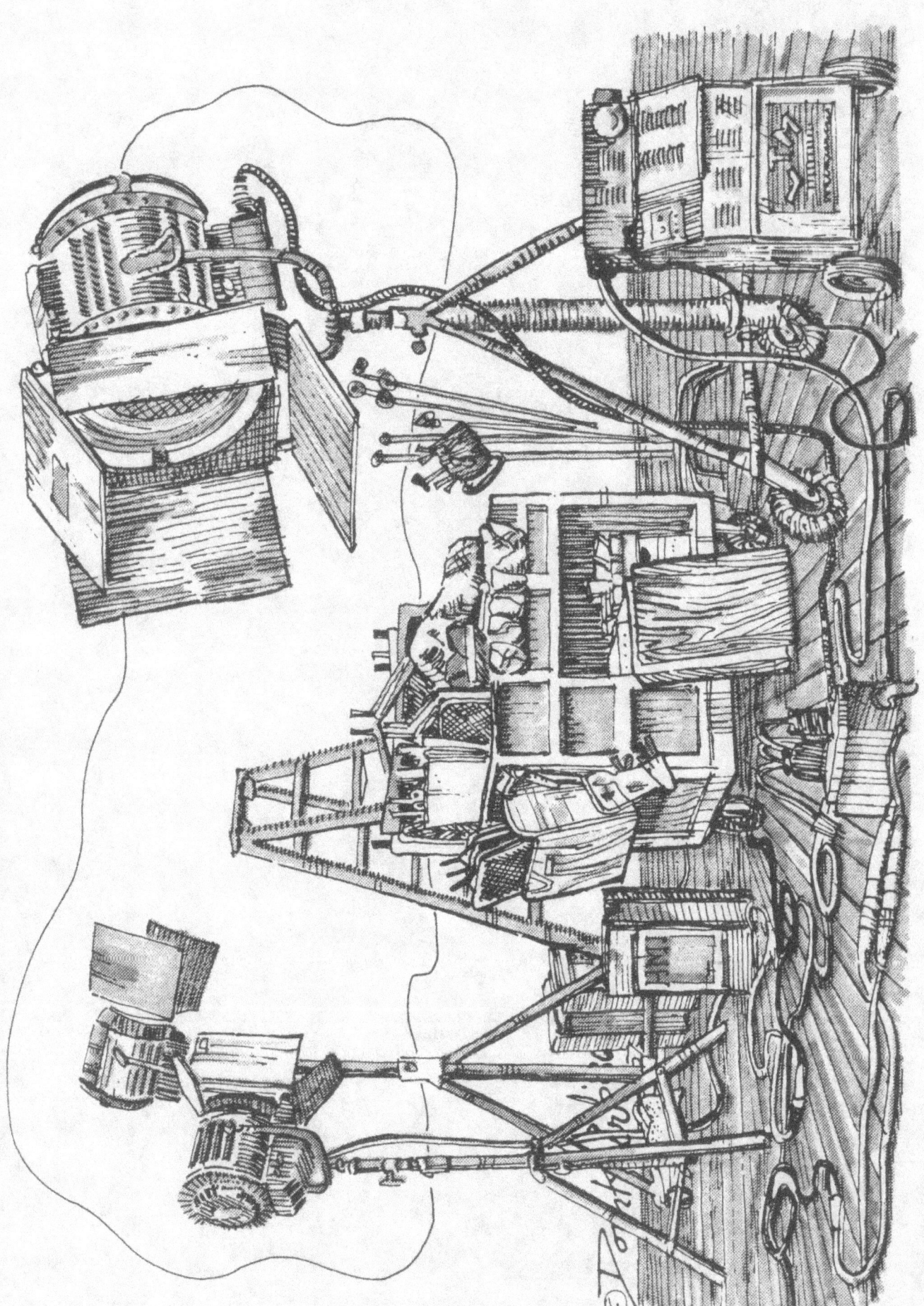

Motion Picture Grip And Lighting Equipment

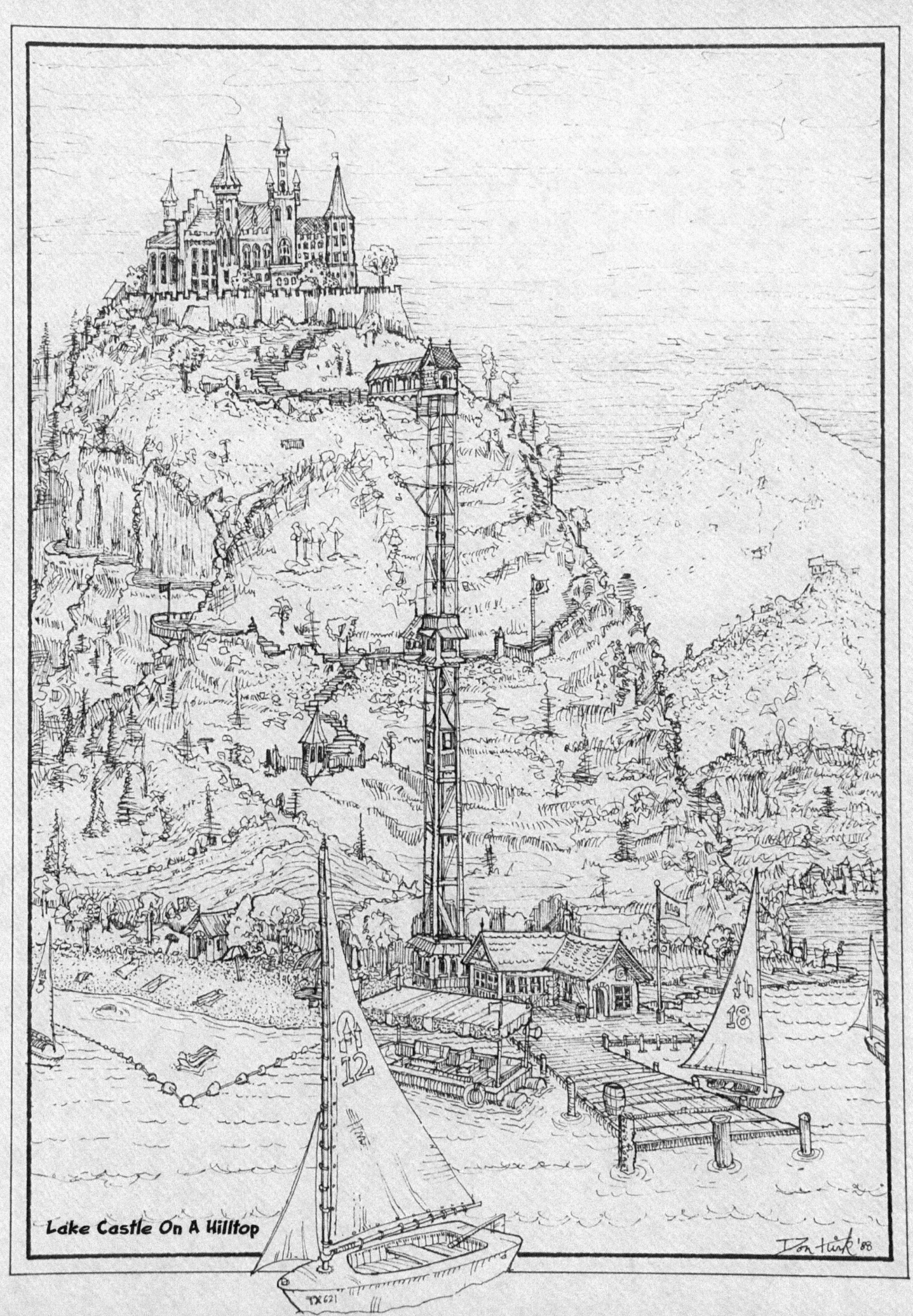

Lake Castle On A Hilltop

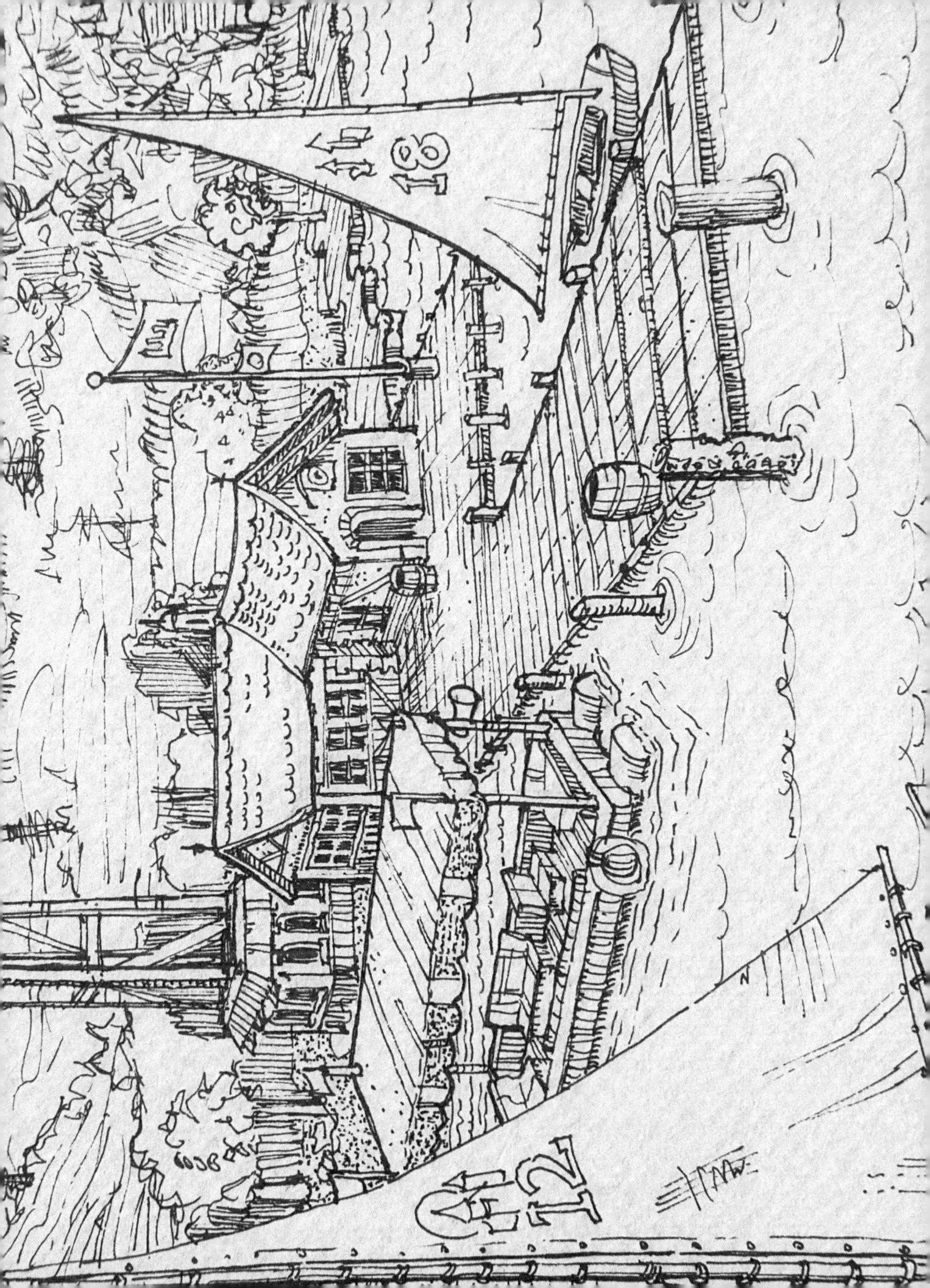

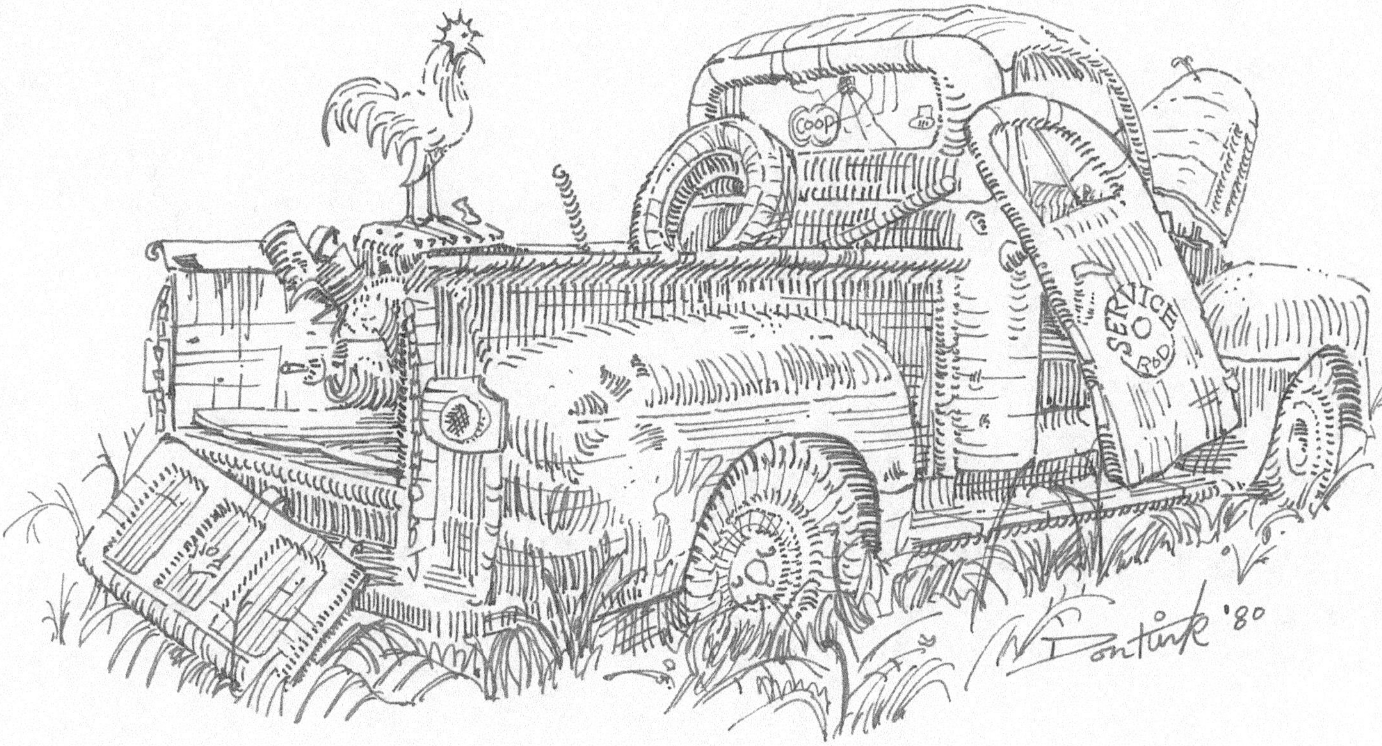

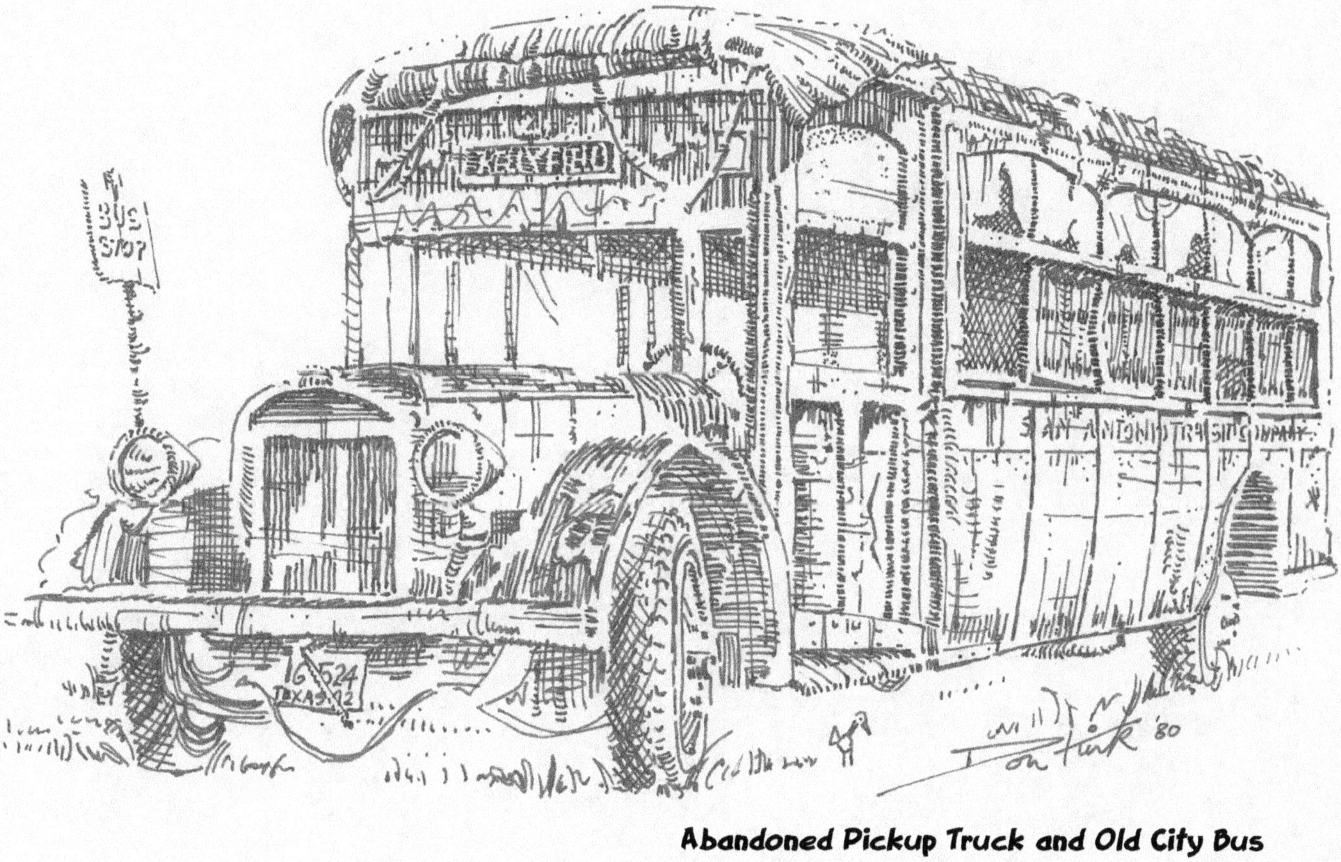

Abandoned Pickup Truck and Old City Bus

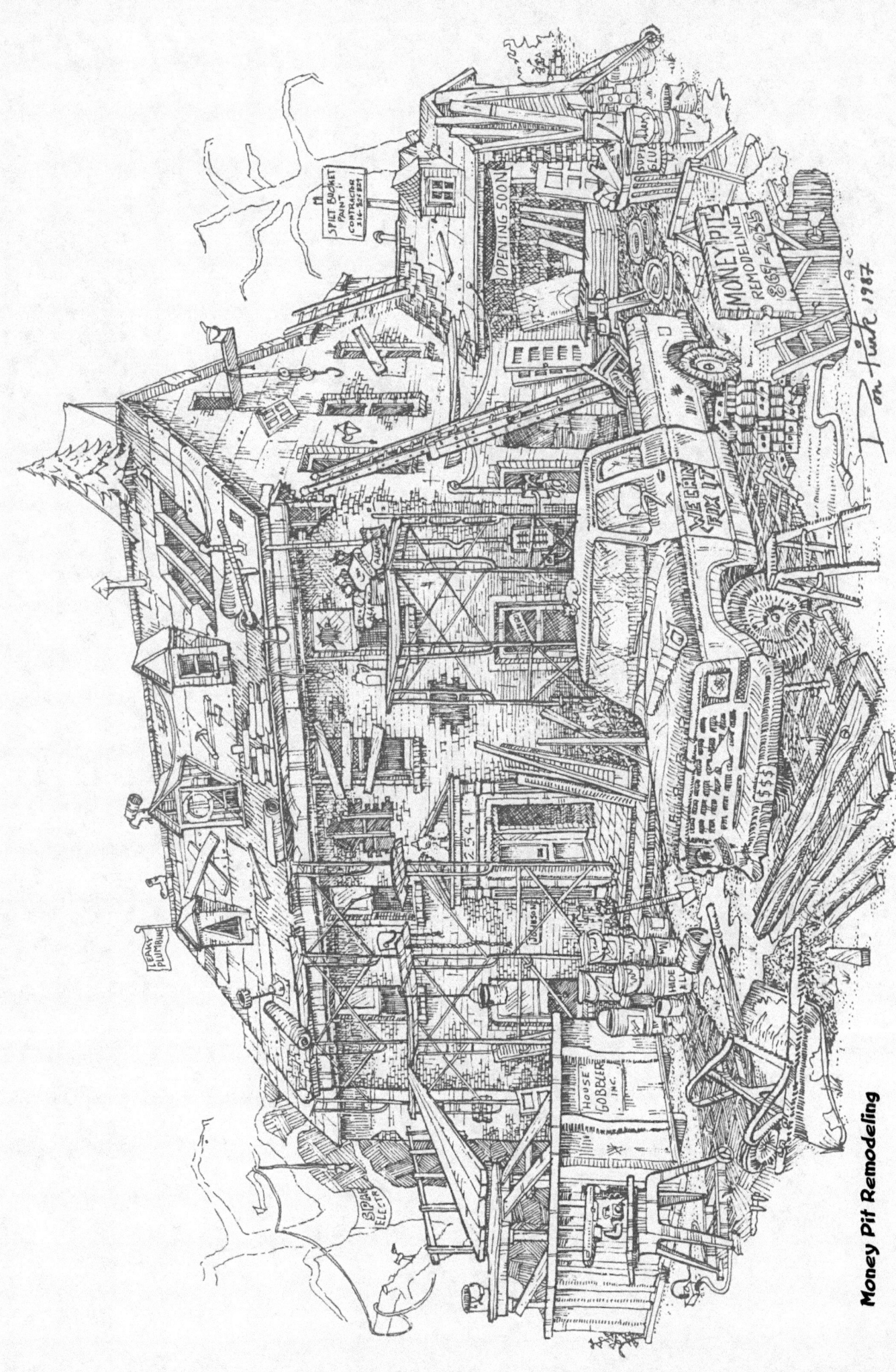

Money Pit Remodeling

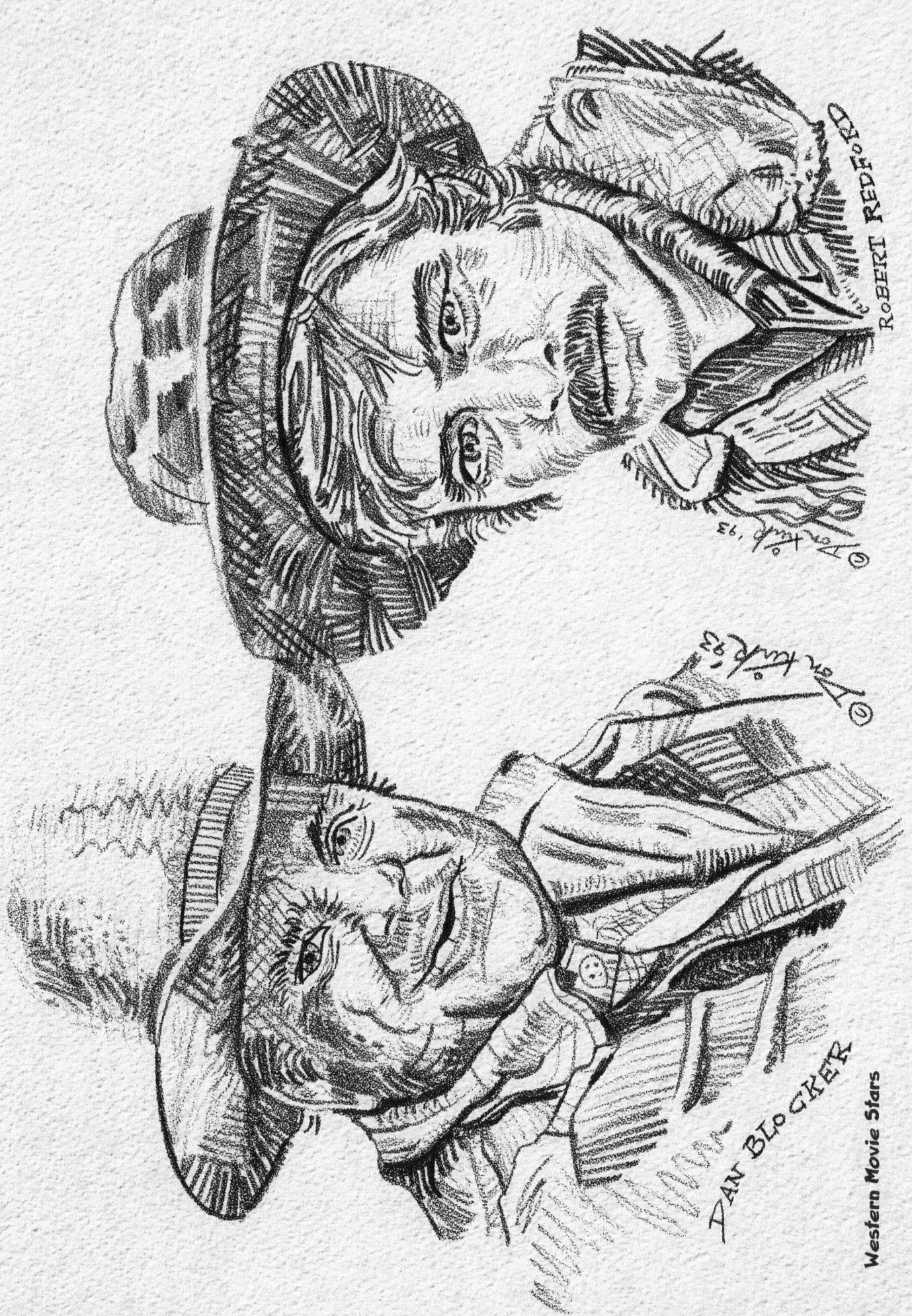

ROBERT REDFORD

DAN BLOCKER

Western Movie Stars

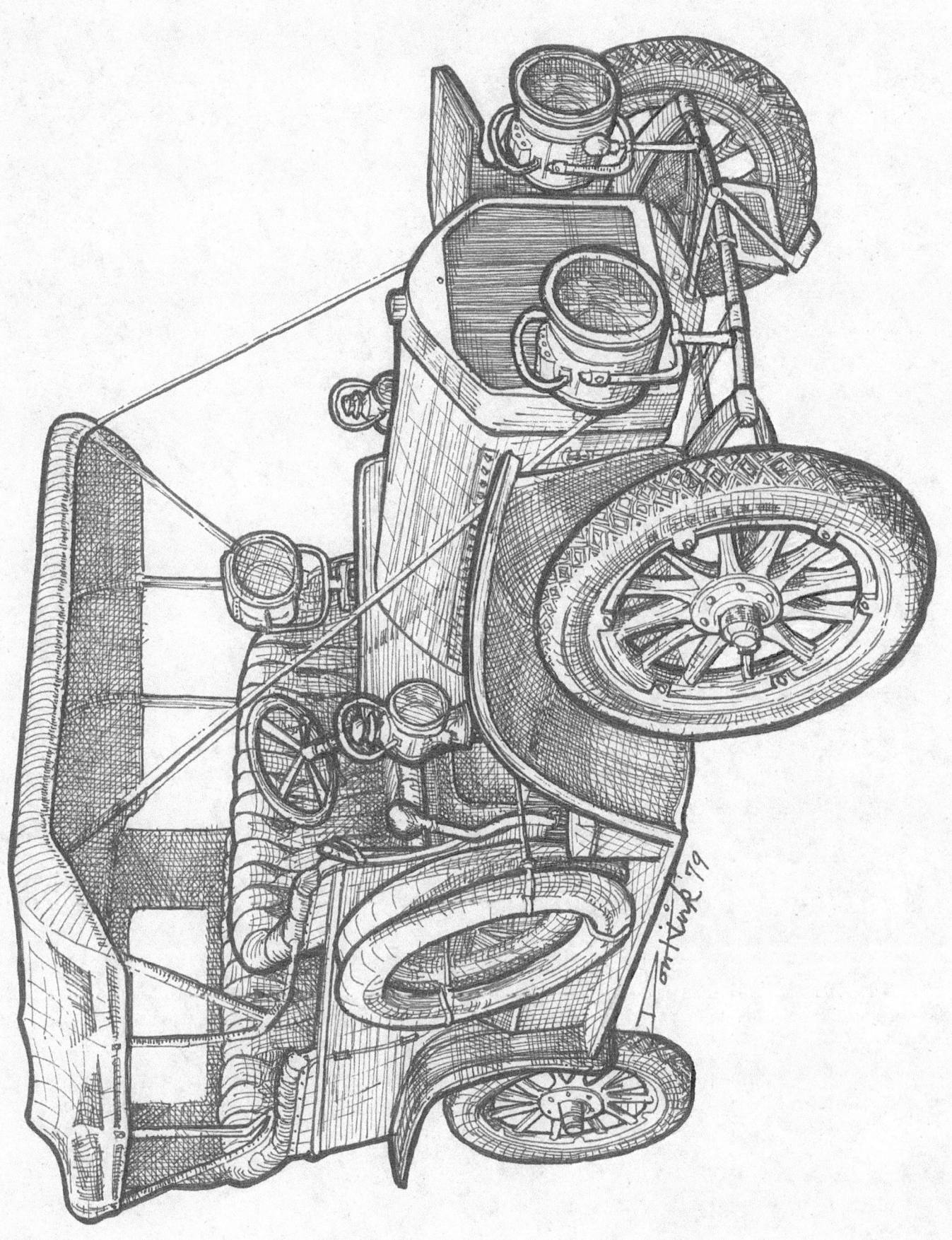

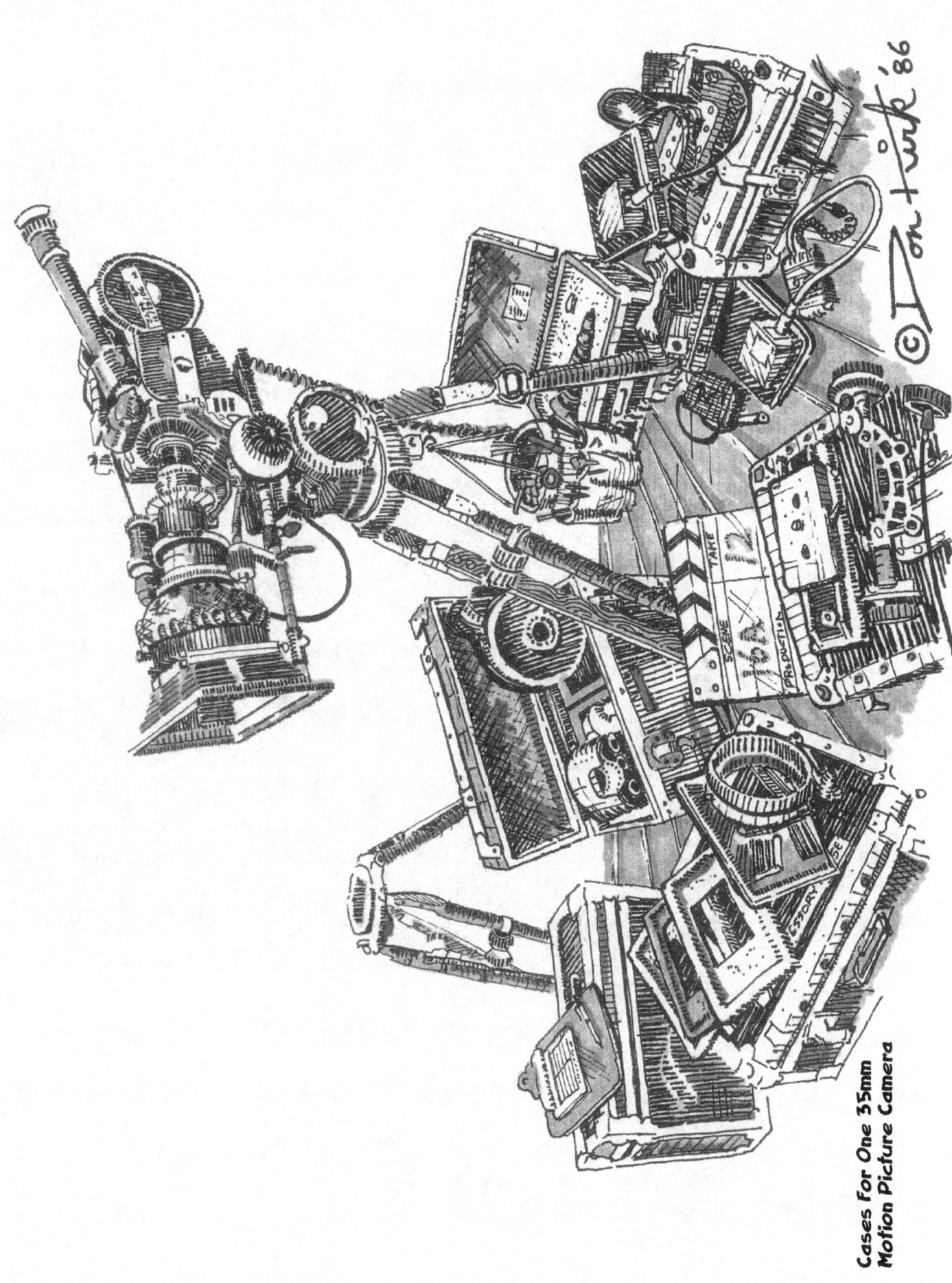

Cases For One 35mm
Motion Picture Camera

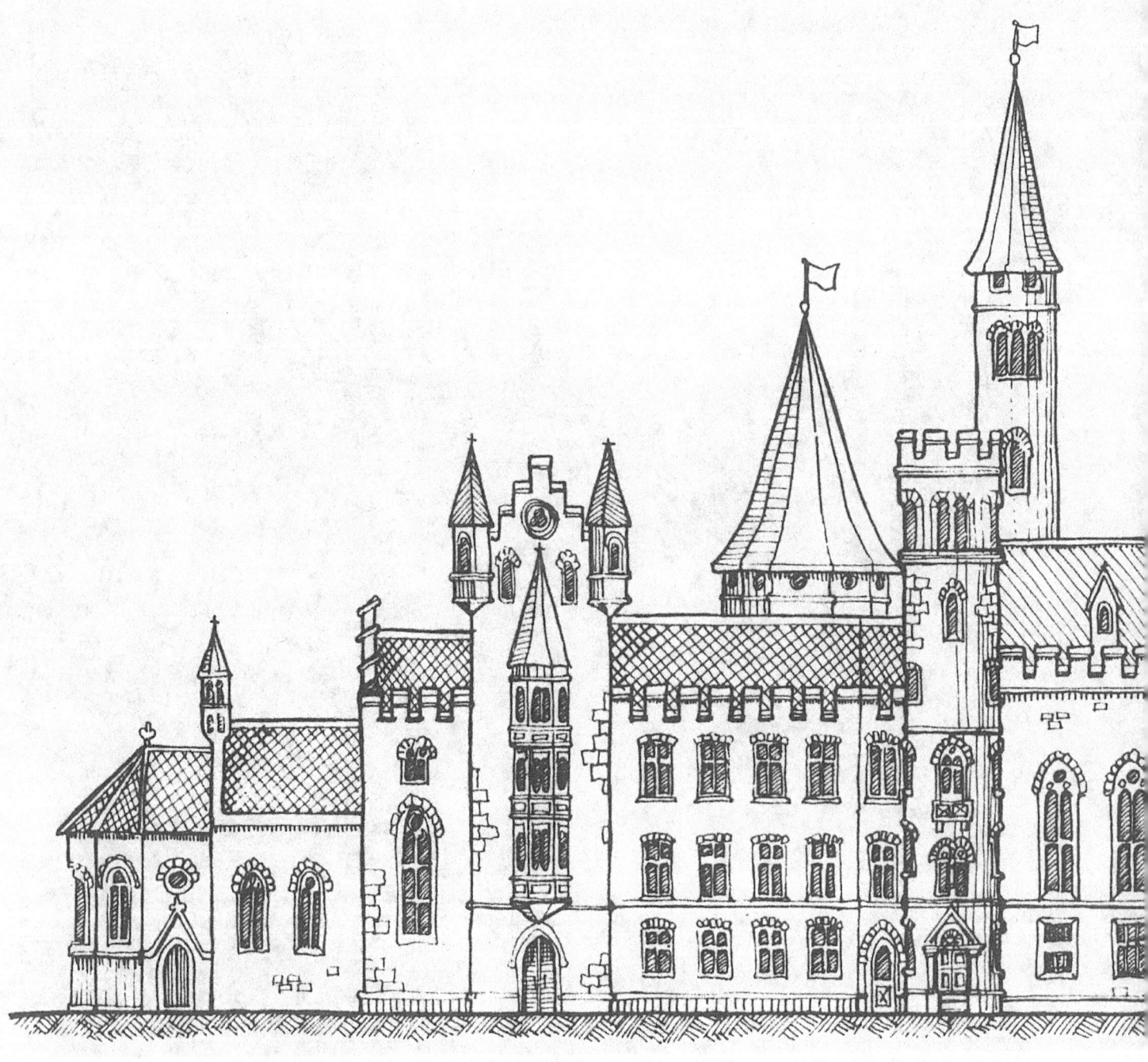

ST. MICHAEL'S CHAPEL

QUEENS DRAWING ROOM

ROYAL APARTMENTS (KITCHEN BELOW)

STAIR TOWER

COUNT (TREASU

HOTEL SUITES
DUNGEON WAX MUSEUM
(BELOW COURTYARD LEVEL)

MEDIEVAL HISTORY LIBRARY

BANQUE
DINING A

Hohenzollern Castle

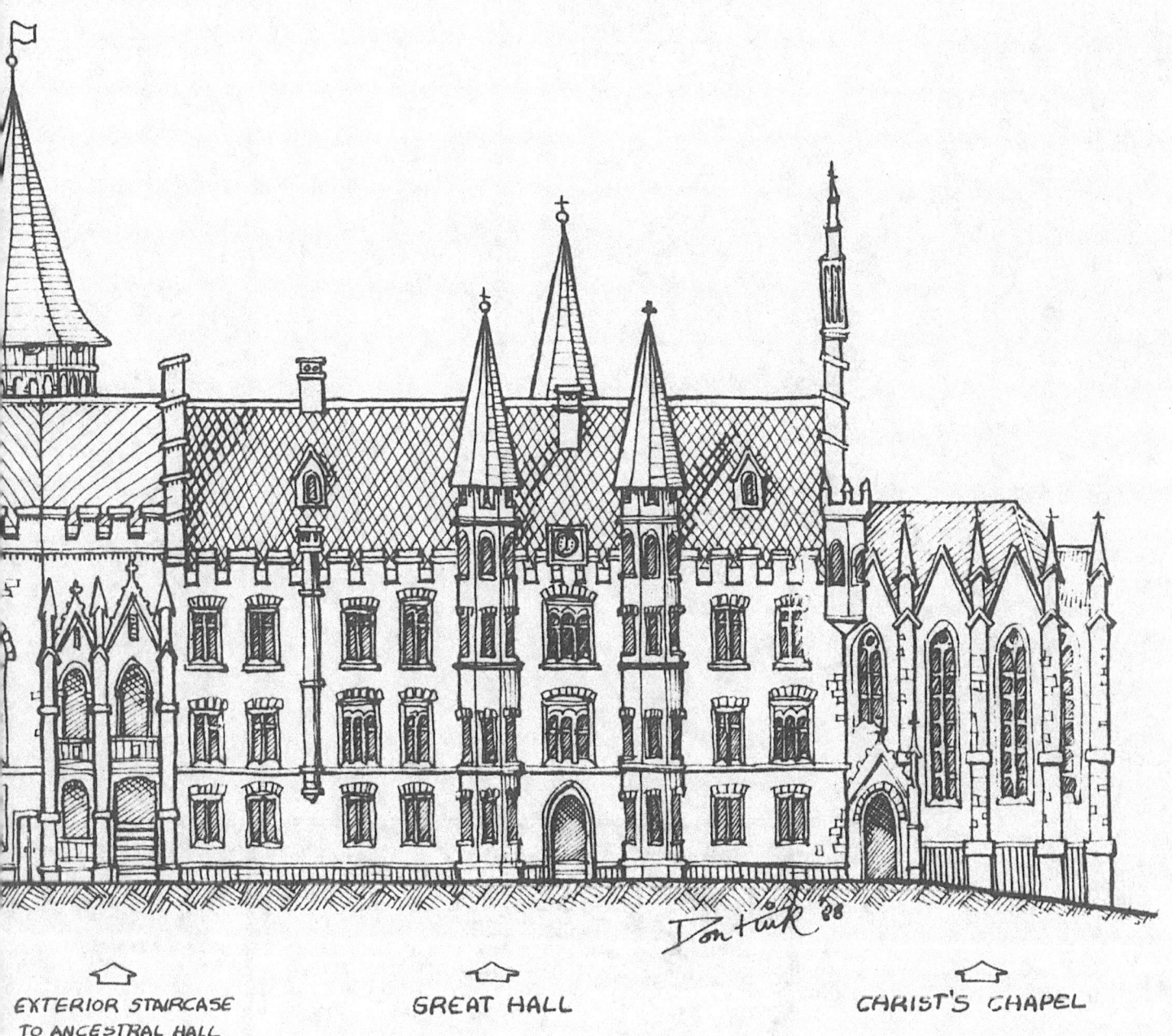

EXTERIOR STAIRCASE
TO ANCESTRAL HALL

GREAT HALL

CHRIST'S CHAPEL

MEDIEVAL
WEAPON AND TOOL
MUSEUM

HOTEL ROOMS
RESTAURANT

NON-DENOMINATIONAL CHURCH
FOR WEDDING CEREMONIES

COURTYARD ELEVATIONS

DRAWING BY DON KIRK

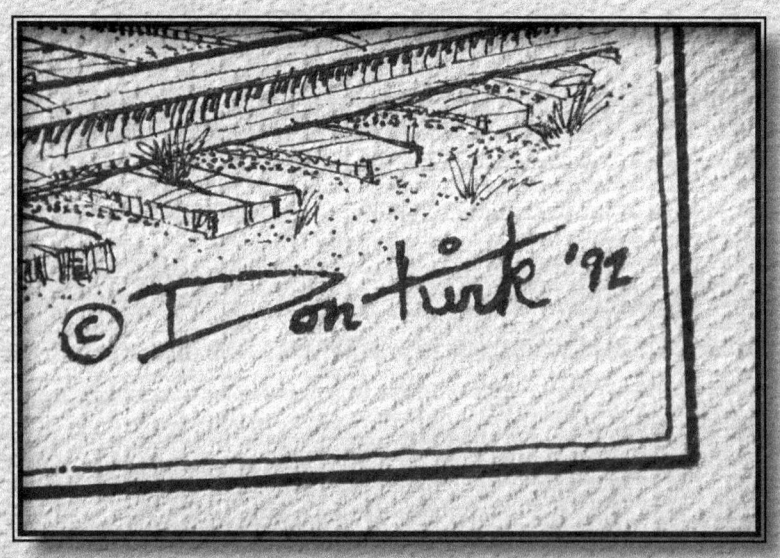

© Don Kirk '92

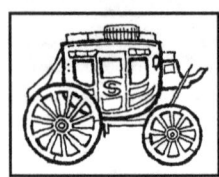

ISBN 978-0-9898004-7-1

90000

9 780989 800471

www.ingramcontent.com/pod-product-compliance
Lightning Source LLC
Chambersburg PA
CBHW080951170526
45158CB00008B/2447

* 9 7 8 0 9 8 9 8 0 0 4 7 1 *